BY THE BANKS OF THE NESS

BY THE BANKS OF THE NESS

Tales of Inverness and District

Mairi A MacDonald

Paul Harris Publishing

Edinburgh

First published 1982
by Paul Harris Publishing
40 York Place, Edinburgh

ISBN 0 86228 043 5

Printed by John G. Eccles, Printers Ltd,
Inverness and bound by James Joyce &
Duffin, Edinburgh

Contents

Preface

THE author of these articles, Mairi A. MacDonald, was born in Inverness at the beginning of the century. Her father, who was of an old Glenmoriston family, was a prolific writer on Highland subjects and a collector of folklore and music, as well as being a composer of Gaelic verse. The MacDonald family to which her mother belonged lived in the district of Abriachan on Loch Ness side and was one which produced several pipers.

While a pupil at Inverness Royal Academy during the war of 1914-18 Mairi MacDonald showed that she had inherited her father's artistic temperament when she had her first article printed in the *Weekly Scotsman*. It was followed by others and over the years her work appeared in various journals. From about 1950 to 1975 the *Scots Magazine* published something by her roughly every year. Several papers which she read to the Gaelic Society of Inverness appear in the *Transactions* of that society, of which her father was a pillar for many years. On the Society's centenary in 1971 a short history of it was written by her.

The selection of articles published here first appeared in the *Scots Magazine*, with the exception of 'The Highland Capital' which was a contribution to *The Heart is Highland* (1954).

Note: The interpretation of the place names in Chapter Ten, and in several instances elsewhere, is Miss MacDonald's own.

Chapter One

Inverness When I Was Young

THE face of Inverness has rapidly changed, giving cause for mixed feelings among us townspeople. Not only have we achieved an imposing bridge, but Bridge Street, that narrow, bumpy street of a bygone age has been demolished and rebuilt.

Yet there were some of us who loved that crazy street, the target of so much abuse for a generation trying to negotiate it in high-speed cars. For us it breathed history and held memories. Inside the narrow closes one could explore ancient houses with turnpike staircases where the gentry once had their homes, and enjoyed a leisurely life quite unknown to moderns. It was down Bridge Street that the fugitives from Culloden raced in their mad rush to get away to the hills and safety, and it was in the Queen's House on Bridge Street that Queen Mary resided when she visited the town in the sixteenth century.

Now Bridge Street is altogether different — wide, with modern stores and car parks — quite continental-looking, some say — and no doubt an asset to the town. That Inverness is unsuited to the traffic of the motor age and to the needs of tourism, no reasonable person would deny, yet the Inverness of fifty or sixty years ago had charm and character, and I am glad to have known it.

Inverness then was a quiet town, with a lazy, easy air about its streets, no rush, no traffic, an errand boy pushing a hurley, an occasional cab or carriage rolling along with top-hatted doctor or country gentry, and nothing more startling than the tinkle of a bicycle bell to disturb one's saunter.

One row of cabs was stanced in front of the Exchange, another in the Station Square. These provided all the transport necessary. Gas lamps spluttered their fickle lights in the evenings, lit by a "leerie", and shops remained open till after eight o'clock.

Inverness was a very Highland, very residential town — two facts of which its inhabitants were highly conscious. Socially, it acknowledged four distinct strata. There were the "county" fami-

lies, usually of long Highland pedigree; the professionals —
doctors, lawyers, accountants, and the like, and if any of these
could claim descent from good Highland family, they mixed freely
with the "county"; next came the trades folk and shopkeepers,
many of whom were substantially well-to-do, but thought to be
lacking in the social graces and culture of the other classes; and
lastly, the "working class" and labourers. Social climbing was
considered an ignorant vanity.

One thing for which Inverness was famous was the English of its
inhabitants, which exhibited a distinctness of accent and clearness
of articulation not to be found with elsewhere in Britain. Strangely
enough there was little Gaelic spoken in the town — the aftermath
of the "Forty Five", followed by a deliberate policy of eradication
in the schools having gone far to kill the language. This was
something which worried my father and many of his Gaelic-
speaking friends, who made it their business to revive the language and its music.

A very genuine interest on the part of the townspeople resulted,
Gaelic concerts and societies becoming extremely fashionable and
well attended. Who can forget such singers as Kate Fraser, Jessie
MacLachlan, Kenny Macrae, and Rory MacLeod, who made
names for themselves not only in London, but also New York?
Gaelic became incorporated in the curricula of most secondary
schools, and was accepted as a certificate language. Personalities
such as Alex. Grant, leader of the Strathspey and Reel Violin
Society, Johnny MacDonald, king of pipers, and Mrs Logan, of
the Highland Orchestra, made Highland music popular everywhere.

Friday nights, when we had no lessons to prepare, were
"ceilidh" nights in our home, when the "Gaelic-ers", as we called
them, gathered together in our drawing-room to learn old Gaelic
songs. My eldest sister — a Mod Gold Medallist — accompanied at
the piano, while we listened, entranced, to fine voices singing
what was to us the loveliest of all music. What delightful evenings
these were — my father fingering the intracacies of the old music
on the notes of his chanter, so that the singer could catch each and
every grace note. My mother humming the Gaelic words. The
singers putting everything they had into the songs! Radio, TV,
they don't compare!

I vividly remember the excitement caused by the appearance of
the first car, even though I myself did not see this marvel. It was

owned by Dr Kerr, a local practitioner. My brother had been in town when it passed, and rushed home, wide-eyed with amazement to report, and held us all enthralled as he described how a man with a red flag walked in front clearing a way for the vehicle — and on it rolled, all on its own, no horse, no one pushing — just a man seated behind a steering wheel and guiding it. It was wonderful!

We did not, however, miss motor cars, for we loved travelling on our own Highland Railway line, which had opened up an easy way to the magic of our Highlands. One could run down to Nairn to sea-bathe, or visit Strathpeffer, with its medicinal springs, baths, and wells. Who could fail to be impressed by Novar, with its Black Rock or Devil's Gorge — an awe-inspiring chasm nearly two miles long and over a hundred feet deep?

We loved, too, the run where the train left Daviot station and descended by a graceful curve into the valley of the River Nairn. Beyond the wooded ridge rose the Ross-shire mountains, with Ben Wyvis as centre-piece. The Great Glen opened on the left, terminating at Mealfourvounie, that beautiful dome-shaped mountain on the west side of Loch Ness.

Shopping was fun — for our shops were mostly run by towns-people, multiple stores scarcely having appeared. I often accompanied my mother on her rounds and met other mothers — and mothers were regal and impressive in these days, with their Gainsborough hats, and well-tailored costumes with ankle-length skirts which swished their importance.

We usually started off by visiting the fish market, where fisherwives in traditional dress — wide, dark-blue woollen skirts, Shetland shawls crossed over in front, leather waistbelts provided with a special pouch to hold their knitting needles, and mutches on their heads — sat on forms behind tables on which were boxes of sparklingly-fresh fish and Nairn "speldings", which once tasted could never be forgotten. My mother often talked of how these women had lost their husbands and brothers in one night, in a dreadful storm, and praised them for their independence, earning their livelihood as they did. They seemed to me as a child to have beautiful, kind faces, soft voices, and exceedingly fine hands. These last were due, my mother said, to the oil which seeped into them from the fish.

One of the most fascinating shops was a jeweller's — Fraser, Ferguson & MacBean. Here, I admired, in addition to endless expensive jewellery, the clan crests and kilt ornaments — the work of skilled silversmiths who plied their craft in the basement of the premises.

There was one shop, however, I was not too keen to visit — "Caber's" shoe shop. Here were stocked most beautiful brogue shoes — the pride and glory of the proprietor. Here, too, our shoes were repaired, and that was the rub! No sooner did my mother express her desire to see some shoes for me, then "Caber" gave a sly wink, and the banter started, in a mixture of voluble Gaelic and English.

"Oh-ho-o, so this is the wee 'isean' (brat) that kicks the toes out of all her shoes." Then addressing me, "Why can't you look where you're going, instead of walking all 'spad-chasach' (splay-footed), and knocking your heels all 'cuagach'? (off the level). You don't deserve to get shoes. Sit down till I see what I can do for you' — and off he trotted to the back of the shop to 'burach' (search) amongst his piles of boxes, much to my relief. Then, as we left, my new shoes parcelled up, a parting shot — "And see and take care of these, or I won't give you another pair, ever."

Then there was Donald MacKay's bookshop, where we bought our school-books. This gentleman laughed his whole way through life — nothing ever causing him a serious moment. His bookkeeping was hopeless, accounts always inaccurate, and when ours arrived on one occasion much higher than it had any right to be, my father set off, full of righteous wrath to give him a bit of his mind.

There was no surprise, no apology — just laughter, and "As you say! As you say! The fact is when I see the name MacDonald in my books I always think of your bairns. They're the nicest bairns that come into my shop." My father, completely mollified to find his brood so highly thought of, forgot his anger, and all was fun and games once more. Years later we realised that this was our wily bookseller's stock excuse to every irate parent.

There was, too, the mouth-watering fruit shop owned by the parents of the late Gordon Daviot, the playwright. Here on occasion Gordon's mother — not unlike her illustrious daughter, but rather smaller — attended to one's wants, a running commentary coming from her husband most of the time. I always felt I travelled the world in this shop — for no sooner were apples chosen, than Mr MacKintosh's husky voice regaled us with — "All the way from Canada, these"; oranges "from sunny Spain";

bananas "from the Tropics"; dates "from Africa"; and glorious melons "from Salonika". Often after I grew up, I met people who insisted that no fruiterer in Britain could vie with Mr MacKintosh for quality and selection.

Inverness bristled with churches of every sect and creed — Established, United Free, "Wee Free", Wesleyan, Episcopalian, and Roman Catholic. These sects were to some degree all censorious of each other. There is a story told about one of the Protestant ministers and a Catholic priest which illustrates this. These two gentlemen met on the Suspension Bridge, the priest jocularly addressing the minister thus — "Now, if the devil were to come here just at this moment, which of us do you think he would take first?" The minister's ready reply was, "Me, of course, for he's got you already." Among Roman Catholics, I suppose the roles would be reversed!

In the "Wee Free" manse, the blinds were never raised on the "Lord's Day". All preparations for the day were completed on Saturday evening — three tables laid for the day's meals — and no milk delivery allowed on the Sabbath.

For all denominations the day was a solemn occasion. Most families walked sedately to church in the morning, fathers stiffly raising tophats, mothers bowing graciously, and children giving tight little smiles as friends were acknowledged en route. Some indulged in walks in the afternoon, but most remained quietly in house or garden.

We were not allowed to sing or play the piano. Visiting was taboo. Sunday was a day of rest!

There were several schools in the town, ranging from free to private. We, like most of our friends, attended the Royal Academy — a fee-paying, co-educational school, whose rector was my father's friend, Dr W. J. Watson. All sorts of pupils from the other schools eventually drifted into ours, the only one with staff and equipment adequate for preparing pupils for the Higher Leaving Certificate.

Many of my generation will remember Charlie Greaves and these lines:—

"Chasing Charlie Greaves,
Hitting him with peas,
We shall come rejoicing,
Chasing Charlie Greaves!"

Charlie Greaves was a science master — woefully short-

sighted. The boys often took peashooters into his class and
amused themselves by shooting peas at the back of his neck.
Because of his eyesight he could never catch the offenders. We
had Prayers in the hall every morning, when a chapter was read
and a hymn sung. When "Bringing in the Sheaves" was the hymn
chosen, these lines were substituted by us and sung with great
gusto!

Of great importance to us were the children's concerts,
arranged by our singing master, Mr Roddie. Mr Roddie came to
Inverness from Glasgow, and was often referred to as "the man
who made the Highlands sing" — for it was he who introduced
Curwen's Sol-fa method to all the town and rural choirs.

Every Christmas there was an "At Home" for pupils in the
school hall, whilst former pupils held a ball in one of the local
hotels. Often while I was wriggling into my best party frock, our
home was invaded by my elder sister's friends who had come to
have their hair done by a French lady, who circulated amongst
several families — ours included — giving lessons in French
conversation. This "coiffeuse par excellence" arrived complete
with hair-nets, hair-pins, small hair-pads, combs, slides, curling
tongs and much other impedimenta.

Complete confusion was the usual result — so it was with very
great relief that I watched my sisters and their friends go to town
one year to have their hair done at the "Maison Victoria" — a
ladies' hairdressing salon. This was a new venture in Inverness,
the first of its kind. It had been started by a young townsman
who, having gained an M.A. degree at Aberdeen University,
thus threw overboard the possibility of a teaching career. There
were those who considered this very foolish, but how wrong they
were, for this was the man who invented the MacDonald
permanent hair-waving system, and amassed a fortune, from
which a bursary has been established in his memory at Aberdeen
University designed to benefit a student taking Honours in
Mental Philosophy — a subject in which he was deeply interested. A large sum of money from his estate has also been
gifted to the Trichological Institute for research on diseases of
the hair.

During the summer months we often went to The Islands of an
afternoon to listen to Herr Meny's band. This was a German
orchestra splendidly attired in Hussar-like green uniforms,
heavily braided on cuffs and collars. Mr Neil MacKintosh of

Raigmore had been foremost in securing the orchestra, and Mrs Gordon-Cumming was one of the patrons. One was indeed lucky if these two happened to be present, for in addition to a delightful programme there was the thrill of Mrs Gordon-Cumming tossing a rose to Herr Meny, as he bowed his appreciation at the end of the performance. He unfailingly caught the rose, and blowing her a kiss, pinned the flower to his tunic. This was considered very Continental behaviour!

The Games, in the Northern Meeting Park, in September, were a highlight of our lives. The whole family attended them, my father and brother in Highland dress. My father usually joined the piping judges in a small tent on the field, whilst the rest of us watched the events, announced by the raucous voice of Donnie Dallas.

After September we began to look forward to the sharp frosty days when we would be skating on Loch na Sanais. With skates over our shoulders we ran and slid along the Donkey's Lane — now Mayfield Road — down Godsman's Brae, over the swinging Infirmary Bridge, up Ballifeary, over the Canal Bridge, and there was the ice, already crowded with a medley of townsfolk. One corner was fenced off for curling, and here the very raw hung on the wires, emulating Mr Winkle at his worst.

Tourists, in that far-off Inverness I remember, were almost all well-to-do. Shooting tenants who arrived early in August to enjoy the "Twelfth", were the main visitors. They could afford to rent estates and lodges, bring personal servants with them, and hire others locally.

How different things are today. Many of the houses we knew as the homes of our friends have become hotels and boarding-houses, and even so, Inverness is taxed to accommodate the thousands who flock into the town every day in summer.

We had our odd characters in my Inverness. "Cackie Eppie" was a damsel of uncertain years who flounced around our streets in a billowing Victorian frock, ornamented with all the odd bits of rags she could sew on to it. She didn't care "a hait" for anyone — police included. When errand boys called her nickname after her, she gave chase, brandishing a short stick and sending them flying.

There was also Johnson — The Maggot Poet. This gentleman — two bandy legs supporting a round, rum barrel body, topped by a round moon face escaping from a small seaman's cap, rolled

navy-like along our pavements, thrusting his poems — a penny
per printed sheet — into our hands. Were they doggerel or
ultra-modern?

"There's no grass that grows so green
   As the grass that grows on the Maggot Green."

or

   "See the fly upon the steeple
   Looking down upon the people"   ʹ

Whatever they were they gave many hearty laughs to our
townsfolk — and our poet seemed to thrive.

Chapter Two

Keeping the Law in Inverness

IN the early stages of society justice was administered to the inhabitants of a township from some outstanding hill or eminence. In Inverness the hill chosen was Tomnahurich, world-famous today for the beauty of its cemetery.

Legend connects the origin of this hill with St. Columba, who is said to have turned his boat upside down on its site, and thus laid its foundation. Tomnahurich certainly does present the well-defined outline of an upturned boat.

In the year 1514 Lord Thomas Lovat held his court there. He issued a decree setting forth the prices of food, clothes, shoes, cattle and timber, and regulating servants' wages in the town.

There was as yet no jail in Inverness. Evil-doers received rough and ready justice. A slanderer might be punished by branding on the cheek with a red-hot iron of the fleur-de-lys — a device adopted from France — or by "lugging to the trone" (having an ear nailed to a beam). He was probably obliged to attend church, where the malicious lie was admitted and the delinquent made to say "False tongue, she lied", or to wear "the branks", a bridle consisting of a headpiece and a sharp iron which, entering the mouth, restrained the tongue. Banishment from the town could follow in more serious cases.

David I had made Inverness the seat of Government for the North of Scotland in 1135, and thereafter all cases concerning property "challenged for theft" were brought there. These cases were examined by the reigning provost and his burgesses. To gain the status of a burgess it was necessary to possess at least one rood of land within the burgh. By 1557 the council consisted of 13 members. They were assisted by a number of officials — one or more town clerks, a treasurer, a procurator-fiscal, a dempster, tasters of ale, comprisers of fish and flesh, who fixed prices and saw to it that the food was sound, comprisers of biggings (build-ings), "liners", who decided boundaries and measurements, messengers, burgh officers, the town crier, masters of work, and the "custummars", who collected Customs.

Three chief courts were held every year, at Michaelmas, Christmas and Easter, and here business of a very diverse nature was enacted. Heirs were served, burgesses entered; stallangers authorised to trade, tanners, cordiners (shoemakers and leatherworkers), litsters (dyers), bakers, fleshers, brewers licensed; prices of commodities fixed; the town's lands and fishings let; civil and criminal actions heard and disposed of, and rioters, assaulters, slanderers, thieves and immoral characters punished.

The policing of the town was done by the burgesses and in-dwellers, who were legally bound to watch and ward. This was no idle duty, as all classes, even field-labourers, carried arms, and were not slow to use them.

Imprisonment as yet was comparatively rare, though there was a Tolbooth in existence where the provosts and burgesses held courts, a purpose for which it proved quite unsuitable, according to a reference of 1561, alluding to an intention to build "one cunsall house to the towneschip".

There is no record of the precise date when prison sentence became part of the law, but there is an interesting story concerning a Tolbooth prisoner of the seventeenth century. Cameron was a renowned cattle-lifter, and followed his avocation with such skill that the sheriff had to imprison him. Sentence of death followed his conviction, and into the Tolbooth he was thrown to await execution.

By sheer force, however, he broke out, and fleeing to the banks of the Ness, hid in a cave, becoming a greater threat than ever to the surrounding country. From the entrance to his cave he commanded an extensive view of the narrow pathway which bordered the loch-side, and seeing the sheriff riding along this route one day, he seized him and threatened his life if he did not agree to reverse his sentence and declare him a free man. The sheriff had no choice but to comply, and on the following day, true to his word, publicly proclaimed Cameron a free man. Cameron reacted worthily to his reprieve by becoming a law-abiding citizen and rearing a large and respectable family in the precincts of the town.

In 1685 when the stone bridge spanning the Ness was built, a vaulted room was included in its third pier to serve as a prison. Near the wall of the bridge was a trap-door, and a few steps down from it an iron door from which was a descent of a few steps more into the prison itself. This was only six feet high, with an area of a little over ten feet by seven feet. On the sides of this room were a stone seat, a small window, and two apertures to dip for water.

A letter written about 1720 by two of its occupants shows what the conditions were. They complained of being "shut up close and exposed to all the rains from heaven — enjoying little or no shelter." Often they were waist-deep in water and afraid of being drowned. The prison was tight and narrow, and so infested by rats that they were weary of trying to keep alive, and could not hope to last long if not removed to some better place.

The old stone bridge had, however, a happier chapter in its history. Turner, the artist, considered it so beautiful that he sketched it, with part of its adjacent scenery, and an engraving of the resulting picture was used as a frontispiece in an early edition of Scott's *Tales of a Grandfather*.

The Tolbooth at Inverness had the reputation of being "the most dirty and offensive prison in all Scotland". In September 1709 the town clerk paid for a cart of peats to be burnt in it to remove the bad smell. Thirty years later the magistrates gave orders for an iron spade to be bought and given to the hangman for cleaning the Tolbooth.

This illustrious building consisted of a tower, with a wing to the west of it, built of stone. It contained a room for debtors with a window twenty inches by six, a courtroom, and a "thieves' chamber" for criminals. Neither of these prison rooms had a fireplace. In 1690 a stone spire was built upon the tower, on the battlements of which spikes for affixing the heads of criminals were placed.

Inverness, the circuit-town for seven other counties, constantly petitioned for a new jail as the very offensive room in which the criminals were lodged actually opened into the court, where, on occasion, the judges were almost overcome by the smell — but all in vain.

Much "pomp and circumstance" attended the arrival of the Lords of Justiciary at Inverness. This took place twice a year, in April and September. The procession was headed by the town's officers. Then followed the provost, bailies, town councillors, Established Church ministers, and the Sheriffs of the Northern Counties, the latter wearing court dress swords. Then followed the trumpeters, mounted, then the judges in a close carriage, drawn by four grey horses, with outriders in scarlet jackets and buff breeches.

Sentences were extremely severe. By order of the court three boys were banished to Botany Bay. Their offence was that they had appropriated a few coppers from the collection on the Seceders' Church.

On one occasion an Inverness merchant, convicted on extremely slight evidence of receiving a few stolen handkerchiefs, was sentenced to death. Several of the townsfolk feeling that the punishment was monstrously severe, plotted to help him escape. Confined in the "Thieves Chamber", he feigned illness and was allowed to hang sheets around the bare stone walls. Some instruments were smuggled into him, and with these he loosened a few stones behind the sheets. The night before the day fixed for his execution he escaped through a hole in the stonework and fled to the wilds of Strathglass. Eventually he emigrated to America, where he was joined by his family. There he rose to affluence and distinction.

There was, however, a worse prison than the Tolbooth. A letter written in 1709, from John Sinclair, who was imprisoned in the vault of the steeple, provides a description of the miseries endured there. He tells of how he has "suffered sorely for three years", with neither candlelight nor fire, no matter how ill he felt. The prison is so cold and obnoxious that he wonders he is still alive. When the wind blows "more than ordinary, it blows out his candle, and whirls the clothes off his bed, and when it rains he has to change his bed twice or thrice each night in the dark to escape the constant drips, and when there is a snowstorm, floor, bed, and bedclothes are covered white with snow, whilst in frost he has to endure excruciating cold" — so much so that he beseeches the magistrates to allow him to be shifted to the Tolbooth!

By 1791, after further petitioning, a new jail was erected almost opposite the old Tolbooth. Outwardly this was an elegant building, but the internal arrangements left much to be desired. The cells were dark and dismal, situated on the ground floor, and opening into a corridor facing the street. At the west end was the Police Court. The benefit of this especial type of building was that through the corridor conversations could be indulged in between passers-by and prisoners.

In 1845 a small police force was organised in the town. This force consisted of a thief-catcher and three officers, the principal of whom, "Supple Sandy", was the terror of the town. The jailer, nicknamed "White Hattie" because of his headgear, was a strict guardian, nevertheless there was frequently a grotesque conviviliaty.

Market days were gala occasions for the prisoners, who, while exercising in their corridor, threw out lines from the windows, to which passers-by attached delicacies. One enterprising "buddy", Peggy Raff, kept a stall just opposite the jail, where oatmeal bannocks, cheese and, in season, boiled salmon, costing one penny per pound, could be procured.

The fish market was held close to the pavement in front of the prison, and occasionally some practical joker fastened fish to the lines. Sometimes, however, the fishwife herself was attached. Her distressed cries, as she felt herself being hauled up into jail quickly attracted "Supple Sandy", eagle-eyed and fleet of limb, who drove the boisterous crowd away.

The prisoners had a weekly dance. To achieve a really enjoyable evening one had to square "White Hattie", and this was best accomplished by a generous "deoch-an-doruis". There were usually a number of debtors in custody, and these were permitted certain liberties, one of which was to take in whisky, and, "White Hattie" won over, the other prisoners were allowed to join in.

The visitors to this stately function, having collected a fiddler, arrived with a generous supply of whisky. When this was exhausted, an empty bottle and a small bag containing money were lowered to a messenger from a public house, conveniently situated in a close at the back of the jail. It did not take long to get the bottle filled, and returned, and this process was continued throughout the entire evening. "Supple Sandy" seems to have turned a blind eye, perchance two very "blind" eyes, on the whole proceedings.

The foundation of a new county jail, situated on the Castle Hill, was laid in June 1846. Today yet another prison, situated at Porterfield, is the place of detention for delinquents — a modern well-equipped building. A police force serviced with fast patrol cars has taken the place of "Supple Sandy" and his two assistants. Traffic controls, zebra crossings, fingerprints and all the rest of it leave no place for such as Peggy Raff, "Supple Sandy" and "White Hattie" or the fishwives. Perhaps we have lost a certain picturesqueness — but our viewpoint probably depends on which side of the law we are!

Chapter Three

Inverness as a Seaport

IN ancient times Scotland's trade was exceedingly limited; yet there are good reasons to believe that even then Inverness handled a notable part of this trade.

It possessed an excellent natural harbour; it was on the cross-roads of trade — a most convenient mart for export and import exchange; and it was able to supply magnificent timber for shipbuilding. A charter granted by William the Lion conferred on the town the Royal forests which then surrounded it. These forests were truly exceptional. Tomnahurich, for instance, was once covered with immense black oak trees, twenty feet in circumference — the ideal wood for shipbuilding.

Between the years 1643 and 1645 Captain George Scott built a ship "of a prodigious bigness" at Inverness, skilled carpenters from the South being hired for the job, and the timber taken from Glenmoriston. Scott took his frigate to the Mediterranean and, entering the service of Venice, became vice-admiral of the Venetian fleet and the terror of Mohammedan navigators. After his death the Venetians erected a marble statue to his honour, near Rialto, which was seen and described in 1659 by the author of the Wardlaw M.S., Master James Fraser of Phopachy.

In one way we have to thank the English for wakening us up to the tremendous possibilities of our harbour. It was in the area near the harbour that Cromwell, between the years 1651 and 1656, built his fort. When the tide recedes there is still, plainly discernible, the cutting of a new channel engineered by the soldiers under General Monk, who were stationed in the fort. It extends from north of where the fort stood, in an easterly direction, and was intended to cut off the long tortuous channel of the river forming the approach to the town.

In 1675 the oldest part of the harbour, capable of receiving vessels of from 70 to 80 tons, was built at a cost of £300, which was defrayed from the shore dues. Prior to this there was no artificial harbour or pier of any kind. So rapidly did trade now expand that in 1738 it was found necessary to build the New or Citadel Quay, designed to take vessels of 150 tons, at a cost of £2,790.

The letter-books of Baillie John Steuart, so ably edited by the late Dr William MacKay, give an excellent picture of sea-trade in Inverness about this period. Before 1700 and for some forty years after, Baillie Steuart was one of two dozen Inverness merchants, all men of good family, who traded extensively both at home and abroad. He himself owned about a dozen ships — none over fifty tons — and his friends a similar number; so that, in all, some three hundred small ships must have been continually employed by these gentlemen. These little vessels sailed wherever there was trade to be got — through the tide races of the Pentland Firth; across the Minch to Stornoway; over the North Sea to Holland, Norway, Denmark and the Baltic ports; round Gibraltar to the ports of the Mediterranean and the Adriatic.

Wages for crews varied from twenty to twenty-five shillings per month, a master receiving about six pounds for a short "home" voyage. Ships sailed mostly in convoy, and they and their cargoes had to be insured against the Swedes, whose privateers scoured the Baltic and the North Sea, and against Moorish pirates who were the scourge of the Mediterranean and the Atlantic coasts of Morocco, Spain and Portugal — penetrating sometimes even into British waters.

In 1717 one of Steuart's ships, the *Alexander*, Thomas Greig master, sailed for Cork, laden with herring, with instructions to dispose of her cargo there, and then proceed to La Rochelle for wine and brandy. She sailed along the East Coast until she reached the North Foreland, when she was captured by a Swedish privateer, whose commander was an Englishman named Norcross. Norcross started with his prize for Gottenberg, but, landing in France, was apprehended and sent back to England. The privateer continued its voyage without him, but off the coast of Norway, Greig and his Inverness lads attacked and overcame the Swedes and ran the vessel into a Norwegian harbour.

A Danish warship then claimed her as a prize and took her to Copenhagen. Here, with the help of the British Ambassador, the ship, her crew and cargo were released, and in 1718 Greig returned in triumph to Inverness, having sold his herring, not at Cork but in the Baltic!

Smuggling — "free trading" or "fair trading" as it was popularly called — was universal in Scotland, especially after the Union. From Holland, France and Spain luggers brought their contraband cargoes of wine, tea, cambric and brandy. No crime was so respectable as "fair trading", and none more freely indulged in. Gentlemen of rank and position joined the smugglers in their war with the Excisemen. Bailie Steuart and his merchant friends in Inverness took their share in the trade, and the Highland lairds and Hanoverian officers who purchased their wines from them knew all too well that no duty had been paid.

The ordinary perils of the sea took tremendous toll of these ships. Within seven years Bailie Steuart lost five, the *Good Success*, on a blind rock off the coast of Sweden; the *Alexander*, on the Atlantic coast; the *Marjorie*, in a storm near Copenhagen; the *Ann*, off Ushant; and the *Agnes*, returning from a smuggling expedition to the West Coast, was wrecked in the Orkneys.

So brisk did the shipping industry become that in 1765 Mr Baillie of Dochfour and Mr Dyer of London, procured the site of Cromwell's Fort for the erection of a rope and coarse cloth manufactury. This at first consisted of a range of wooden buildings, and when they were burned down stone factories were erected. Here first-class sailcloth was manufactured, and the industry became one of the most lucrative in the town.

In 1804 smacks began to ply regularly between Inverness and London, for the first seven years going once in three weeks, and afterwards once in ten days. Hugh Miller describes these as vessels with large single masts, massive and tall as that of a frigate, and mainsails of a quarter of an acre. The voyage seems to have taken from ten to fourteen days.

By 1812 the Highlands possessed a complete system of roads, of services by sea, and the advantages of communication by the newly constructed Caledonian Canal. In 1815 it was decided to build the Thornbush Pier on the north bank of the river, and rebuild in part, and deepen, the old harbour at a cost of £3,300. The pier could now accommodate vessels of 300 tons.

As late as 1819, however, piracy was still a hazard of the high seas — but now the privateers were American. One of these, the *Blockade of Rhode Island*, with Manly Swat as commander, captured off Cape Wrath, the sloop *Six Sisters*, of Inverness. The *Blockade* was something to reckon with, being about 200 tons burthen, mounted with eighteen long nine-pounders, two twelve-pounders, and one thirty-two pounder in the middle of the main deck. Her master, for all his terrifying name, seems, however, to have been less of a cut-throat than most in his profession. Among his many captures was *The Experiment*, of Dumfries, which, laden with timber, was heading for Beauly. The master of this vessel was sick; and hearing this, Manly Swat sent his own surgeon on board to bleed the unfortunate man. Then, taking all her charts, books, two muskets, a spyglass, and some coals off the vessel, he allowed her to depart.

Shortly after this Munro's shipbuilding yard sprung into prominence on account of the many fine vessels that were being turned out there. In 1828 there were three notable launchings within a very short time of each other. The *Caledonia*, much admired for her beauty and the excellence of her workmanship, was intended for London and Inverness trade; a similar smack for Inverness and Leith trade took to the water several days later, to be followed by a brig and schooner launched almost simultaneously. Schooners were also launched from the yards of Stewart, and Morrison and Lawrence, who were other well-known builders.

The middle of the nineteenth century brought the "iron-track" into the Highlands — the Highland Railway; and now the sea was no longer the most convenient road to Inverness. This new road soon began to cater competitively for trade — so much so that an 1870 Town Directory lists only five ship-owners and five merchant-traders in its pages. There were still shipbuilding yards — Cook's and Munro's on Shore Street; Stewart's at the Citadel, and many small boat-builders — but the back-bone of the sea trade was broken. Seamen (many retired) tenanted the houses of the district near the harbour, which now boasted an inn and a brewery, and had lost much of its seafaring atmosphere. In time the shipbuilding yards closed down to give place to a single repair yard at the Thornbush Slipway.

The shipping history of our harbour would be quite incomplete without mention of the Patersons, that famous family of pilots extending over four generations, of whom the present Chief Constable of Inverness is a descendant. At one time there were eight of these Patersons in "action" — and "action" is the word. There was keen competition for pilotage. The pilots waited in cold or heat, calm or storm, telescope to eye, watching for the first sight of an incoming ship. Then, full speed into their rowing boat, and off to meet the vessel and get the job of piloting her into harbour.

Before the first world war these pilots were divided into two classes: the Inverness pilots and the Beauly pilots, the Beauly No. 1 pilots being the only seamen capable of piloting ships up the Beauly Firth. Familiar to all who frequented the harbour in these days was Daniel Paterson's famous cutter, the *Ban Righ* — "The Queen" — which was later wrecked off the coast of Brittany. Daniel was one of the Beauly pilots.

During the first war both groups of pilots were taken over by the Admiralty and motor boats introduced. After the war ended seven men remained in pilotage. Today these seven are reduced to three — William, James and William, all descendants of Sandy Paterson, the original Inverness pilot of four generations ago, and grandfather of Alexander Paterson, Craigton, both of whose parents were Patersons, to whom I am indebted for this information.

Chapter 4

Changing Patterns of Life in Inverness

I can still see the spare, immaculate figure of our tailor, in his neat, dark-grey suit, bowler hat on his head — for he wore a bowler hat even when working — tape-line hung round his neck; pins in his coat lapel, as he huskily shouted one's measurements to his daughter, who officiated somewhere behind the closely-drawn curtains of the fitting-room.

There followed several fittings, choosing of buttons and linings, and finally the day when to the door came a small boy bearing an immense, black, shiny, oval, plywood box, the lid held secure by a thick leather strap. In this lay, shrouded in layers of tissue paper, the new outfit, and the bill, with the tailor's compliments — £4.

To say that our town has changed almost beyond recognition since my young days would be the understatement of the age. This town was the Highland Capital, and looked every inch of what it purported to be, with its solid stone buildings, pleasant, un-crowded streets, and shops full of quality wares.

As I meander up Bridge Street, along Church Street and towards the Post Office on Queensgate, and view all the concrete and glass architecture, I am sore put to it to think where on earth I am — Tel-Aviv or Bangladesh? The never-ending trail of cars, taxis, caravans, articulated lorries, ambulances, town buses, country buses, furniture vans, sheep trucks, biscuit vans, tractors and sausage vans is a poor substitute for the quiet streets and clear skies of my youth.

It may be objected that my view is a one-sided one, but it is pleasant to look back on an era when our homes were much more lived in than today. Most of the family homes of my old friends are now boarding-houses or small hotels — and the only flower on their lawns is that hardy annual, the "Bed and Breakfast" sign. Then, young folk usually had their own "glory-hole" — an attic at the top of the house, where they could do more or less as they liked, and enjoy the company of their chums.

Mothers had their "At Home" afternoon parties about once a month, when they welcomed any friend who cared to call, and exchange news and views about fashions and most of the local happenings. House dances were very popular — and it was at these that many local romances had their culmination.

Preparations for a dance were simple. Drawing-room carpets were rolled up, floors waxed, a pianist hired for the evening, and a "running buffet" provided in the dining room. "Sit-ooteries" were fixed up in attractive corners of the hall, and if there was a conservatory, this, too, was brought into use. It was a perfect setting for romance.

"Society" in Inverness reached its yearly pinnacle in the Northern Meeting Ball (following the Northern Meeting Games), a very dignified affair, run more or less for the county, by the county, and the cream of the town's higher ranking citizens. Inverness had always been a class-conscious town, a favourite resort for retired army and navy personnel, and those returning home after service abroad. Early in their history (these balls were instituted in 1788) they catered only for Highland lairds and their families, and as these were nearly all related, were private rather than public assemblies.

The best of relations can prove boring at times, however, and more than likely this is what led to the circle eventually being enlarged to include certain carefully-chosen outsiders. The night of the ball was a gala night in the town, large numbers of the citizens gathering outside the Northern Meeting Rooms to watch the ladies and their escorts arrive.

There was also the ball held by the Inverness-shire Volunteer Companies. These consisted of an Artillery Company, the Highland Rifle Volunteers, and the Inverness and Highland Light Infantry Militia. As might be expected, this was a very gay affair with a piquant army flavour about it — the various uniforms giving a colourful background to the proceedings.

In 1871 the Gaelic Society of Inverness was formed. In the early part of the nineteenth century there had been a considerable influx of country people into the town. These people were almost all bi-lingual, speaking, if not writing, both Gaelic and English fairly well. Inverness townsfolk had little interest in Gaelic, its leading citizens and much of its populace being non-Highland, with no knowledge whatsoever of the Gaelic tongue. Indeed, to admit to a knowledge of Gaelic was to admit to inferiority — a country bumpkin amongst cultured English speakers.

It was to remedy this state of affairs and save the beautiful song and literature of the Gaelic language that the Gaelic Society was brought into being by some of the homesick, country-bred youths, who were making their mark in the town and were soon to be amongst its leading citizens. To them it seemed ridiculous that information regarding Highland subjects could be obtained only from the Gaelic Society of London, founded in 1777. Contrary to expectation, the society's meetings and concerts became extremely popular and were largely attended, as were the yearly dinners which were an outstanding feature of this movement. It published papers given by members, under the title, *Transactions of the Gaelic Society of Inverness*. The society, still flourishing, celebrated its centenary in 1971.

There were many among the older country people whose English was not nearly so good as their Gaelic, but, finding themselves in a town where English was spoken by almost all the inhabitants, they felt that they had to do likewise. The result was an odd mixture, with the Gaelic idiom introduced into their English. There was a piquant flavour in the injunction, "Donal, put your nose round the door and see if it's raining". Neither "a trouser" nor "a scissor" ever became a pair, and the Gaelic way of asking a question by making a statement was very common — "You wass ivver in Ooban?" The manner in which two elderly grannies greeted each other with, "Oh lassie, it's me that's pleased to see you", was most heartwarming, while the distortion of proverbs, "Don't count your chickens in the air", gave one something to think about.

With little or no education, and but a scant knowledge of English, these incomers were up against very real difficulties, and it is interesting to learn how these handicaps were sometimes surmounted. A friend of our family had an excellent elderly housekeeper who had been with her for years. When she first came there were seven children in the family who all had milk and a boiled egg about five-thirty. Our friend couldn't understand "Big Anne's" method of setting the table. She laid five places, and then heaped several plates, tumblers, eggs and eggcups on the sideboard. When all the children were seated, she cast a quick glance around, then, mumbling to herself, "Oh, hee — no egk!" promptly laid the extra places from her supply on the sideboard. The solution to the problem presented itself when "Big Anne's" niece paid a visit and explained how the dear soul had never learned to count beyond five.

The Inverness Scientific Society and Field Club, established in 1875, was a society mainly of amateurs, who devoted to scientific pursuits only so much of their time as they could spare from their ordinary vocations. They published records of their work in volume form, which, in the early days, was edited by James Barron of *The Inverness Courier*. One of their earliest excursions was to the vitrified fort of Craig-Phadrig, and it is interesting to note that a "dig" has lately been carried out there under the auspices of the society, which yielded little more information than these old-time scientists had already acquired, except to date the fort as being about 2150 years old.

In the early days there were no cinemas, the usual entertainment being a concert held in the Music Hall in Union Street. The hall would be superbly decorated for the occasion, with a programme extending to something around twenty items. As often as not, a short opening address was given by Willie MacKintosh of Raigmore— an enthusiastic patron of all musical activites, whose stutter did not prevent his being loudly acclaimed!

There was that magnificently-attired Highland violinist, Andrew MacKintosh, who always turned his back on the audience when he began to play, and the intrepid leader of The Reel and Strathspey Society, Mr Alexander Grant, the "second Scott Skinner", who made a habit of hitting his pianist sharply on the head with his bow, "to put him going", before starting to play. If the lady soloist who sang *Bonnie Wee Thing* turned the scales at something over fifteen stones — well, she had a lovely voice!

At a later date the Mod concerts introduced beautifully-trained choirs into their programmes, and many of their soloists, such as Roderick MacLeod and Kenny MacRae are spoken of with enthusiasm in the town to this day.

Several of the town's ministers came from families outstanding in church circles for their zeal and erudition. In 1898 the Rev. Gavin Lang, a cousin of Cosmo Lang, Archbishop of Canterbury, and brother of the Very Rev. Principal Lang, of Aberdeen University, was appointed to the West Parish Church. He had spent twelve years of his life in Canada, and brought a fresh wind into the parish, and, indeed, into much of the town's administration. His son, Matheson Lang, who felt the stage could influence Christianity as much as the church, became one of Britain's leading actors.

With Mr Roddie in charge of the choir of the Free High Church, and Mr Whitehead training the choir of the Old High, the Choral Society was instituted — and from then on, classical music was the theme-word of most church concerts. The first production was the oratorio *St Paul*, which was followed up the next season by *The Messiah*, sung by a choir of about one hundred and fifty voices, and accompanied by a full orchestra.

The family of the Rev. Mr MacEchern were, all twelve of them, very gifted. Acting, singing, writing, these were their interests, and their performances were in great demand. In 1907 the Rev. Donald MacLeod, B.D., was inducted to the Old High. He was a son of the manse, and descended from a long line of famous ministers. His cousin, Dr Norman MacLeod, had held the charge at an earlier date. A handsome bachelor, witty, friendly and very able, it was said that a considerable religious revival took place amongst the ladies of Inverness after his induction!

There was always a bit of sly off-taking of the Wee Free ministers of the town, and many were the jokes told about their sermons. A favourite told how one of their ministers was just about to launch into his harangue when his eye caught a young couple capering in the gallery. He stopped dead, and then bellowed, "When you two in the gallery stop flirting, I'll begin!"

I once met a man who told me he'd spent the longest Sunday of his life in Inverness. He arrived on a Saturday, around lunch-time, and was greeted by the proprietor of his hotel — a jovial, friendly soul, who made him very welcome. About 4 p.m. that afternoon he met his host again — a completely changed person, steeped in gloom, who kept his eyes averted, and silently, almost furtively, passed him by. Meeting a maid-servant, he enquired if anything tragic had happened. "Oh, no, sir", was the answer, "The master is a lay-preacher in the Free North. He's always like this when he's preaching on the Sunday".

Next morning the house seemed deserted. A pot of tea and boiled eggs awaited him in the dining room, but there was no service. He crossed to where a piano stood and strummed a few notes to try to cheer himself up. A head appeared round the door. "If you please, sir, we don't play the piano on the Sunday" — and the head was immediately withdrawn.

Soon church bells were pealing, and he saw his host depart,

walking with slow, measured, restrained steps, as though his feet were covered in corns. He made up his mind to follow him, and soon found himself at an austere-looking church at whose door two elders, guarding "the plate", silently signed to him to enter. His host was in the pulpit, and the congregation, all seated, were droning out a psalm, led line by line by the precentor.

This finished, all stood and remained standing during a prayer which lasted for quite twenty minutes. Thereafter followed a "hellfire and thunder" sermon, delivered with such sincerity and eloquence that he could not help being impressed. This man was preaching according to the Jewish laws of the Old Testament, and it was evident that to him and his congregation the wrath of God was a very real and a very terrible thing. After the sermon there was another prayer, followed by more singing of psalms and paraphrases.

Back at his hotel a cold lunch, minus service, awaited the visitor. Luckily he had a book in his case, so he spent the afternoon in his bed reading. Hearing the bells pealing, and as there was nothing else to do, he made up his mind to try the High Church for the evening service. Here the notes of an organ welcomed him. On entry he was struck by the beauty of the church, the steps and floor of the sanctuary being of Iona marble, and the choir stalls surrounded by handsome, stained-glass windows. The pews were boxed and cushioned.

The congregation stood to sing the first psalm, and sat or knelt for the prayers which followed. The excellent sermon expounded the forgiveness of sin through the resurrection of Christ. Hymns were sung throughout the service.

Completely confused, he returned to his hotel, where a cold supper and heavy silence awaited him. Next morning he bade his host farewell, and found him cheerful and friendly once more, the gloom quite gone.

We shared, of course, in national occasions, and one of those which stands out vividly in my mind to this day was the church service to mourn the passing of King Edward VII in 1910. This was attended by a huge congregation, most of them attired in the deepest of mourning — black clothes, black ties, black crepe armbands, with practically all the members of the fair sex, heads bowed, weeping copiously into black-edged handkerchiefs. Even I had been provided with a black-edged hankie, but, failing to squeeze out the necessary tears, spent most of the time trying to fold it into a dunce's cap. The solemn organ music, the restrained sad singing of the choir, the heavy aura of gloom which manifested itself everywhere, left a life-long impression that the death of a king was a more or less insurmountable calamity.

As I think of church and the large part church services played in our lives, behind-the-scenes surprises bring up a lively chuckle. My school friend was a minister's daughter, so I had first-hand knowledge. It was the custom, at sacrament time, to house several of the visiting ministers in the manse, and provide them with all their meals. Before their arrival the wives sent what they considered to be suitable provender, usually hens, geese, chickens, rabbits and hares — all undressed. My friend felt very sore about this habit. "Just look at this", she said to me, opening the kitchen door. "I've to do hours here". Through a mist of fluff, down and feathers, I beheld their two maids, an extra woman and most of the family, pluck-pluck-plucking feathers as though their very lives depended on it.

The weekend over, I was surprised to find my friend, considering the circumstances, remarkably cheerful, impatient to let me into the secret of her new mood. On the Sunday, she told me, she felt divine judgment had prevailed.

On Saturday night, when we all were abed, the water tank above the bathroom had sprung a large leak, and the water had poured down the stairs into the visiting ministers' boots which were lined up in a small passage, all beautifully shined for Sunday's ceremonies.

Well, the ministers just couldn't wear their wet boots and had to be provided with an assortment of footwear — galoshes, white gym shoes, carpet slippers, snow-boots — anything which fitted. How then, with this odd attire, were they to get to church? The only answer was in cabs — and thus they had to travel, sneaking into the vestry as best they could, having jeopardised their immortal souls by committing the deadly sin of using the manual labour of others on the Lord's Day.

The other day I was browsing over an old local newspaper, dated 1907, when my eye caught the tailend of a letter signed "Very Irate Gentleman". I began to read from the beginning. The gentleman was very irate indeed — and the reason? Well, whilst crossing our High Street some rude person had rung a bicycle bell just behind him, causing him to jump. This sort of impudence was intolerable and must be stopped! I fell to wondering how often he'd have jumped were he walking on our High Street today, where one takes one's life in one's hands — and well nigh loses it — every time one crosses.

Streets — these were places where, if one met a friend, one could stop and have a little chat. Tomnahurich Street — street of the hill of the fairies — has always fascinated me. It is a very old street, a medley of small shops, small houses, narrow closes and side alleys, a few larger shops and a few business premises. According to my 1869-70 town directory, it has changed very little over the past hundred years. It was here that many of the countryfolk set themselves up in small businesses.

On my first visit to this street I remember standing spellbound in front of a window of what was known as a "huckster" shop. Bottles of castor oil, piles of black liquorice straps, cards of hooks and eyes and white linen buttons, a plate of buns, a few eggs, two pink sugar mice and a grey-and-white striped cat, which, sunning itself in a corner, whisked its tail over the mice, were the contents of the window. Years later I learnt that this was the "rendezvous" of the "wifies" who came in from the country to sell their produce. They brought "a puckle tea and a cinder" with them, and the shopkeeper-owner obliged by boiling a large kettleful of water and providing a few buns — there was often quite a party!

It was on this street, too, that one got insight into the complicated character of the countryfolk. Coming, as most of them did, from the hard life of the croft, and disciplined by a narrow religion, they introduced a dimension into daily living that was baffling. Great store was set upon being honest, hard-working and, above all, "respectable".

Several of the shops were licensed grocers. It was a long, slow trek for the Loch Ness-side crofters to drive their cattle down the steep slopes and along the road to the Inverness market, and most of the throats got rather dry in the process. The oasis in the desert was one or other of these shops, where one could nip in and out almost unnoticed. Set on a stand in a corner of these beautifully-kept shops was an immense, light-brown wooden barrel with the word "Rum" painted in brown, edged in gold, on its expansive front. The barrel contained whisky, but it was considered much more "respectable" to sell rum — so you labelled your barrels of whisky "Rum"!

A hundred years ago the leading school in the town was the fee-paying Royal Academy and Ladies Institution. In my youth, as the "Royal Academy", it provided the required standard of training for university entrance. Bursaries were granted to pupils from the non-fee-paying schools and nearby districts for entrance to the Upper School. Thus the cream of Highland brainpower was to be found within its four walls. Needless to say, competition was keen, and hard work was the order of the day.

We were proud of our school; proud of our straw "lids", with their blue and gold bands, and, I think, proud of ourselves. We were given large doses of Greek and Latin, and long, trying sessions of mathematics, including analytical geometry; interesting English under a very favourite teacher, "Golly"; useful French and very inartistic art. Science was taught in an odd way. I have a hazy recollection of trying to find the circumference of a circle by trailing clanking chains around the playground.

Food in the town was always of excellent quality — much superior to what we have today, and quite inexpensive. Country crofters brought in their fresh, "free range" produce, and the surrounding farms contributed the best of home-fed meat, eggs, milk and cream. The indigenous Highland people were tremendously proud — never admitting to poverty. It was something savouring of failure — something of which to be ashamed. "Haining" (economical) in their ways, they managed to make ends meet, and that sufficed.

There was little or no crime, and no vandalism. The most common delinquent was the gentleman who stotted about, having had one or two "over the eight" — vainly trying to make his way home. "Kenny the Masher", or some other kindly "bobby", usually took him by the arm and led him to his house, ringing the front door bell before dumping him on his doorstep to be dealt with by his better-half, who "gave him his psalms" and saw to it that he didn't get the chance to disgrace himself again.

Yet, even in 1907 the writing was on the wall for the changes that were to come. A rally of over one hundred motorists, under the auspices of the Scottish Automobile Club, starting from Glasgow and arriving via Aberdeen at Inverness some time around four o'clock in the afternoon, caused a very severe local headache — for this particular day was a Fast Day. Some four hundred visitors were expected, and the town would be wrapped in Sabbath quiet — no shops open, no one to welcome them. In spite of a plea to allow shops and restaurants to open for two hours, from 4 p.m. to 6 p.m., the town fathers remained adamant. The Fast Day was held as usual, and the visitors were allowed to starve.

In November of that year the Town Hall was not large enough to accommodate the people who gathered there to see and hear Miss Helen Fraser and Miss Isobel Seymour, advocating "votes for women". The audience was captivated by the personalities of the ladies, and their cause was warmly supported by Provost Gossip and ex-Provost Ross.

As I wander from street to street, and the heterogeneous crowds from everywhere and anywhere keep milling around me — surprise, surpise — what do I hear? Two youngsters speaking Gaelic! Now that Gaelic is being taught in schools, this is the latest craze! The youngsters speak to each other in a language grown-ups don't understand. We have Gaelic concerts and ceilidh evenings galore, and the kilt is a favourite dress. The Town Hall has had a "face-clean" and winks at me as I pass. "Times change, old girl", it says. "Cheer up! You never know what's coming next!"

Chapter 5

A Steamer on Loch Ness

EVER since that morning of October 24, 1822, when the *Loch-ness* steam yacht, accompanied by two smacks, departed from Muirtown, Inverness, amidst enthusiastic cheering, on her first voyage through the canal, cruising on Loch Ness has been a delight. By 1832 three steamers plied on the canal, one of these, *Highland Chieftain*, sailing on to Cromarty and Invergordon.

Early in the twentieth century a complete fleet of steamers, under the flag of David MacBrayne, sailed our Scottish waters. Some of these, *Cavalier* — Glasgow to Inverness; *Fusilier* — Oban to Inverness; *Glengarry* and *Gondolier* — Inverness to Fort Augustus, were familiar to most Invernessians and tourists.

In recent years no pleasure steamer has regularly sailed Loch Ness. The more welcome therefore was the new arrival, *Scot II**, a 57-ton tug owned by British Waterways, a branch of British Transport. Built in 1931 she was converted from steam to diesel propulsion by Robb of Leith. Her speed was nine knots. The space previously taken up by the boiler was turned into a comfortable lounge below decks, while at deck level an enclosed observation space had been constructed.

Smartly painted in white, blue and yellow, she brought back to my mind a vivid memory of halcyon days, when a sail on Loch Ness was a frequent and most enjoyable outing costing six shillings for fare, and two shillings for a three course lunch or high tea aboard.

The day we went up the loch always started with a mad scramble on the part of us children to get into the cab which waited on our drive. The cabby was an understanding man, and put up with our antics, in the full knowledge that the appearance of our parents would immediately reduce the pandemonium to law and order, which it did — and somehow all four children and two parents were accommodated in that quite inadequate vehicle, my brother

* Sailings began in 1961.

proudly seated on the "dicky," beside the cabby.

All too soon the two miles that lay between our home and Muirtown Quay were covered, the horse jogging more and more slowly as it dragged us up the slope which led to the quay. Then before us lay the *Gondolier*, in all her glory of black paint and scarlet funnel, actually just a midget pleasure boat of about 173 tons — but to us a wonder ship, able and apt for her voyage through waters that held mystery in their depths, and enchantment in their surroundings.

All around us was bustle as the crew, in coarsely knit blue jerseys, bell-bottomed trousers, and sea-men's caps, helped to get passengers, animals, and luggage aboard. A short gangway ran from the pier to the steamer, manned on either side by sturdy mariners who, seeing my mother approach with me in tow — I was the youngest — promptly laid hold of me, and with a "whoops-a-daisy" whirled me through space, and landed me safe and sound at the cabin door.

To me the cabin was a lovely room, with endless windows on each side, all hung with red velvet curtains with tasselled edges. The centre floor, on which was a writing desk complete with inkwell, pens, and postcards of the *Gondolier*, was carpeted in red, the seats running the length of both sides cushioned with red velvet.

There were always lots of people in the cabin, French, German, and others, whom we could not place, but dubbed Americans. To me as a child they seemed dressed in the oddest manner, spring, summer, autumn, winter all at once! Perhaps they'd heard about our climate and came prepared! It was quite usual to see a man attired in knickerbocker suit, short spats, tweed or mackintosh cape and panama hat. The women mostly wore ankle-length dustcoats, large flat hats, and veils tucked tightly under their chins.

On one occasion I remember seeing a very plain-looking lady, most elaborately and expensively dressed, saunter through the cabin. Two Highland women eyed her sarcastically, then one, with a knowing wink of the eye murmured, "She has a dress on her!" "Ay, an' she would need it", her friend replied. At that moment I became aware that my parents were laughing heartily, so I laughed, too, and then the rest of the family joined in. Soon everyone in the cabin was laughing, though I'm sure most couldn't tell why! But that was what it was like on board the *Gondolier* —

friendly, good-humoured companionship and fun everywhere.

At one end of the cabin was a high glass case laid out with boxes of Inverness rock, tartan purses, and dolls dressed in tartan kilts with black velvet tunics and tartan plaids. I usually ambled in the direction of this, with a view to getting my father to buy me a box of rock, a manoeuvre usually highly successful, to the joy of my family. Then, kneeling on our seats, and with faces glued to the windows, we watched as the boat slipped into waters banked with masses of brilliant yellow broom.

The boat progressed past shores clothed in emerald, olive, jade — every conceivable shade of green. The beat of the paddles was music in our ears, as woods and fields seemed to slip farther and farther away, and a wide stretch of water beckoned to adventure. Soon we were at Dochgarroch, and could glimpse Dochfour lawns and house. Next Lochend hove into view; then Aldourie Castle. The loch widened; the paddles beat faster, and there before us was Abriachan Pier.

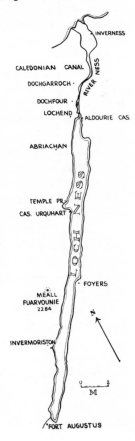

Here we watched for the pierman — a spindly little man who seemed to unearth his moth-eaten red flag from somewhere underneath the pier, and hasten — his haste was quite frantic — to unroll it and set it up — the signal that passengers were waiting to come aboard. We knew this pierman well. He spoke very little English — in fact only one remark, "She's lett the day!" and whether "she" was late or not it made no difference, that remark was wafted on the breeze as we sailed in.

With the new passengers aboard we sailed out and on, hugging the west bank of the loch, and heading for Temple Pier. Low red rocks erupted out of shimmering larch woods, precipices scowled, but here and there a bright green clearing offered a gentler vista. Tiny mountain rivulets cascaded into the loch's waters — and all around the mast wheeled the gulls, following, always following, with their hungry cries, as they swooped to pick bread from the hands of passengers on deck.

A bell sounded — and the rich odour of Scotch broth was around as a chef's boy scurried through the cabin and downstairs into the dining saloon, laden with a huge tureen. At his heels scurried a second, bearing what smelt like a hissing joint, hidden under an immense cover. Yes! Lunch was on! Down we followed in their wake, and were soon seated at a long narrow table resplendent with spotless damask cloth, shining glass and silver.

As we did ample justice to an excellent lunch Temple Pier was reached, and here awaited Sandy Ross — a dour, implacable Highlander if ever was. On one occasion a party of tourists questioned the payment of the two-penny pier dues. Sandy had no time for argument. "Pay yer tuppence an' shut yer mooth", was his withering reply. Next day, however, he received a letter, unstamped, and when he opened it, the page inside read "Pay yer tuppunce an' shut yer mooth". (The penny postage rate was then in operation.)

Lunch over we scrambled upstairs and on to the deck to get a clear view of the towering Meall Fuarvounie, and that wonderful ancient stronghold, Urquhart Castle, its keep and ruined turrets seeming to grow almost out of its grassy mounds. Here haunted the ghosts of kings, courtiers, soldiers, and prisoners done to death in its dungeons. One eyed the grey walls with fearful fascination, breathing more freely as the paddles beat faster while the steamer pulled across the loch in the direction of Foyers.

What a lot there was to watch on deck, too. There, behind a great oak wheel stood the captain. Nearby was the ship's compass in case of polished brass — and wonder of wonders, a circular glass plate through which one watched the engine at work. Here, too, taking the air, was the stewardess, a magnificent figure in stiff black alpaca, starched snow-white apron, and large filled muslin mob cap.

Her splendour rather awed me, I must confess, so imagine my delight when, on one occasion, I beheld a seagull bless her in no uncertain manner. Never shall I forget her expression — consternation! disgust!! rage!!! Then a quick retreat downstairs followed by an unbelievably rapid return — fresh apron, fresh cap; spick and span as ever!

Foyers, reposeful in a half-circle of tawny sands and magenta rhododendrons found us craning our necks over the deck rails to

glimpse the hotel, Dun Deardshuil, and the monument com-
memorating the untimely death of Miss Fraser of Foyers from
heartbreak after the fatal accident to her betrothed, Patrick Grant
of Glenmoriston.

Again the loch was crossed to visit Invermoriston Pier, which
seemed always extraordinarily busy with coal carts, animals,
tourists, and the village worthies. North of the pier we could see
the old house of Altsaigh, and quite near was Invermoriston
House, seat of the Glenmoriston Grants. Voluble Gaelic filled the
air here, and much hand-waving and cheering as we drew away
towards Fort Augustus. Here we disembarked and "took a turn
round" while waiting to re-embark for our return journey.

It was always teatime when we left Fort Augustus, and downstairs we clattered to enjoy hot buttered muffins, and glorious
oatcakes. Somehow the journey home seemed quicker — one pier
after another swinging by, till Dochgarroch was reached and the
crew jumped on land to open the lock-gates. This was an intri-
guing operation. They stuck long wooden poles into what we
called "whirligigs" and pushed these round and round — four
men to each. Slowly the locks opened and on we sailed, slowly,
ever so slowly, whilst the crew jumped back aboard.

In next to no time we were back at Muirtown Quay, being
bundled into one of the waiting cabs — stealing one last long
affectionate look at our beloved *Gondolier*, as we rumbled off,
already excitedly discussing our next trip, for sailing on Loch Ness
was an experience whose delights never diminished.

Chapter 6

Dores — The Village with the Tranquil Air

STRANGE things have happened to country villages over the centuries. Some have disappeared, while others have assumed the vestments of the small town. Dores has done neither, for while it has become a residential suburb of our bustling Inverness, it yet retains its own charm and character.

The road from Inverness to Dores runs for several miles through farm country. Near Dores a steep declivity and sharp bend bring, as if by magic, the wide expanse of Loch Ness suddenly to view — a picture dazzling the senses by its utterly prodigal loveliness. A few yards farther along is Dores — a small "clachan" nestling round its Parish Church.

Dores boasts only one main highway — a short stretch of the modern car road which runs along Loch Ness-side. This stretch is flanked as of yore on the lochside by the Inn, fraternising happily with a few old-world cottages, one of which houses the local Post Office, and on the other side by the school and school-house, the Church, and several modern houses of attractive design. Almost opposite the Inn and Post Office is a considerable settlement of Council houses — the homes of Inverness citizens from all walks of life, who travel daily to work in town. Behind this side of the road lie the farm lands and farmhouses, and still farther beyond rise the friendly hills.

In the long ago Dores and the excellent agricultural country around attracted religious devotees, for there are known to have been several chapels in this area. When, however, the level of Loch Ness was raised four and a half feet by the formation of the Caledonian Canal, much that was ancient Dores disappeared — and today very few vestiges of this early culture remain.

The name Dores is descriptive. There are two schools of thought as to the derivation of the name. The first suggests Dubh

— Ras — "the black wood"; the second has it that in remote antiquity the Church stood on Dores Bay, and in this case the word "Ros" meaning "headland" may have occasioned the name.

The road from Dores to Foyers, on the southern side of Loch Ness, stimulates the choice of Dubh-Ras — for here, to quote Dr MacCulloch, we find "a green road of shaven turf, holding its bowery course for miles through close groves of birch and alder, with occasional glimpses of Loch Ness and of the open country". In May, this "green road of shaven turf" pied with myriad yellow primroses, stretches a carpet of such bewildering beauty that our townsfolk motor out in hundreds, just to see and admire. The closeness of the wood and coppice, yielding still and prolonged vistas, bestows a character of peculiar repose, freshness, and sanctity.

Dores village, with its main thoroughfare, was clustered originally round the Church. The Inn stood almost opposite, with its back windows overlooking the wide stretch of Loch Ness, glimpsing Torr Point, and the wooded parks of Aldourie Castle. Near the Inn stables was the estate sawmill, worked by the Minister's Burn, which ran near the Church. A little way along was General Wade's Bridge, built when he constructed the road along this side of Loch Ness, and near the Torr Gate stood the old meal mill.

For many years a well-known distillery was situated in the vicinity of the old mill. A certain owner of this distillery — a Provost of Inverness — owned a second distillery in Inverness, and also a licensed house. After his death a pipe line connecting the two was found, down which whisky had flowed duty free for many years!

Inside the entrance to the churchyard was "the watch house" — a small cottage which is witness of the panic occasioned throughout Scotland by the practices of those two infamous gentlemen, Burke and Hare. To guard against body-snatching, men were stationed every night for about six weeks after each interment. This, however, did not prove to be the melancholy vigil one might suppose, for nearby, in the dead of night, the old meal mill was often set a-working to grind malt for illicit distillation — and as there was always a fairly liberal supply of the "uisge-beatha" on hand for home consumption, Dores enjoyed a night-life all its own — and a very sociable and convivial one it was. Many were the tales told during these seances — not the least interesting being that of The Old House of Clune.

It was about the year 1776, when young Fraser of Foyers and MacGillivray of Dalcrombie were dining in Old Clune Farm House, then rented by MacGillivray, that a quarrel suddenly arose between them. Dalcrombie seized a bottle and struck young Foyers on the head with it. The latter managed to make his escape by jumping through a back window into the yard, but expired almost immediately. In consequence of this, coupled with bankruptcy, MacGillivray fled to America. It is interesting here to note that this MacGillivray was grandfather of the MacGillivray who succeeded to the estate of Dunmaglass in 1857. He had been a smith in Canada.

Then there was the memory of that proud day when General Wade, having surmounted all the difficulties of the making of the Loch Ness-side road travelled grandly in a coach and six from Inverness to Fort William, "to the great wonder of the inhabitants".

Nor could the sad scenes after the Forty-Five be forgotten. In the retreat from Culloden many of the unfortunate Jacobites passed through Dores, in sorry plight, endeavouring to make their ways to their respective homes. The village inn-keeper proved himself to be a man of rare resource, for in order to relieve the hunger of the fugitives, he put half-a-boll of oatmeal into a large wooden tub, and having mixed it into a dough with water, placed this stimulating food at the road-side, so that they could help themselves to it as they hurried along.

It was at this time, too, that the minister of the Parish, Mr Bannatyne, though at heart a supporter of the Hanoverian succession, put aside his scruples in order to help the unhappy fugitives, imperilling his very life by his actions.

What tales could have been told during these nocturnal sessions — and what colourful characters enliven them! Through the narrow village "street"

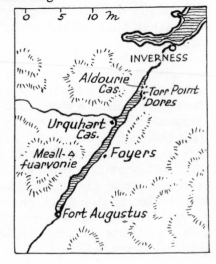

travelled such eminent personages as St Columba, Samuel Johnson, astride his Highland garron, accompanied by Boswell and a servant — also on horeseback, Robert Burns, Coleridge, Southey, Christopher North, Simon Lord Lovat, and Murray of Broughton. In Old Clune House, too, was born in 1765 Sir James MacKintosh, noted statesman, philosopher, and historian.

Aldourie Castle is one of the notable old buildings of the district. It was in 1754 that William Fraser of Balnain bought Aldourie estate from Capt. Barbour. The lower half of the square tower is the oldest portion of the castle, and dates back to 1626. The castle was greatly enlarged by Colonel William Fraser-Tytler and when, in 1850, the tower was raised by two storeys, the stone turrets built, and a cement fireproof floor laid between the ground and first floor, a highly significant event took place, for this very solid floor laid the ghost of a lady in grey who perpetually wandered from the west bedroom to the front room.

In the grounds of Aldourie Castle is the private cemetery of The Fraser-Tytlers — and here we meet something — a surprise. Under the lych-gate, at the side, is a screen, formed of three panels, adorned by bronze sculptures from the well-known paintings of that illustrious artist, G. F. Watts.

It was in July 1886 that G. F. Watts, then aged sixty-nine, asked Mary Fraser-Tytler to become his wife. She agreed, and almost immediately travelled north to her old home, Aldourie Castle, to prepare for her wedding. While there, however, she suffered a great grief, for her nephew, aged three years, fell from his pony and died about a month afterwards. She wrote to tell Watts of the tragedy, and when he replied he enclosed a small sketch of the Angel of Death with a child in her lap, on whose head she is placing a circlet. "Death, the Angel, crowning Innocence" forms the centre bronze of the screen.

In 1900 Watts, feeling in need of rest, expressed a wish to visit Dores. One of the houses on the Aldourie Estate — Dalcrombie — was immediately put at his disposal. A short time afterwards a new craft was introduced to Dores. At Compton in Surrey, the home of the Watts, clay-modelling was taught by them to a number of the younger generation. A branch of this craft was organised in Dores, and the very attractive houses built there for the manager and staff are still to be seen. The kiln was housed in what became later the Village Hall. The clay was brought from the South. Many were the terra-cotta coloured garden urns and vases turned out from this workshop, which eventually produced also the arch for the Village War Memorial — now part of the church gate. The dearth of young workers caused by the first World War forced the project to be closed down.

Despite the introduction into Dores of a small colony of council houses the character of peculiar repose, freshness and sanctity still obtains. It is as if the entire village were an elegant natural monastery, with nave, choir, and several graceful aisles — and into pews, along one of these aisles council houses have quietly slipped and taken their places.

Chapter 7

Rosemarkie and Fortrose

TOWNS, like people, have their ups and downs. They, too, find themselves caught up in the wheel of life, spinning round from prosperity to decline, and then, something altering in society, the almost forgotten place finds itself suddenly basking in the limelight. An excellent example of this is found in those two delightful holiday resorts, Rosemarkie and Fortrose, situated on  the shores of the Moray Firth, about a mile distant from each other.

The name Rosemarkie, or rather Rosmarkyn, is said to be of Gaelic origin — "Ros" signifying a promontory, and "maraichin" — seamen. This burgh is sometimes called "The Point of Ross", because it is the first land sighted by seamen when sailing up the Moray Firth. It was its situation which gave Rosemarkie its early importance.

We first find mention of Rosemarkie in connection with St Moluag. A church was dedicated to, and probably founded by him there, and according to "The Aberdeen Breviary", was his burial place when he died in 577 A.D. The most interesting of Rosemarkie's antiquities, a runic cross, discovered under the flooring of the parish church, was found to cover a crozier or "Bachuil mor", a ring, and crystal ball — the insignia of a bishop. St Moluag was a bishop.

About 1578 the historian, Bishop Leslie, who resided in this district, refers to Rosemarkie as "a veri ancient town" — and very rightly so, for it is said that Rosemarkie was created a royal burgh by Alexander I, King of Scots, who died in 1124 A.D. In the reign of King David I about 1125, the Bishopric of Ross was founded, with Macbeth as its first bishop. A Charter of 1255, witnessed by

several of the clergy of Ross, was given at Rosemarc — apparently
the burgh.

From this date we begin to consider the fortunes of Rosemarkie
alongside those of its neighbour, Fortrose ("Fort," meaning
under, and "Ros" a promontory), whose ancient name was Chanonry. Here, during the ninth century a few monks settled, to lay
the foundation of a very simple Christian organisation. Over the
years this settlement increased, till in 1455 the place was annexed,
by King James II, to the Burgh of Rosemarkie — an event which
clearly denotes that at this period Rosemarkie was the more
important place.

From Mary of Guise, through David, Bishop of Ross, Rosemarkie received permission in 1553 to have a market cross, and to hold
weekly markets on Saturday, and twice-yearly fairs.

Thus, at this date, Rosemarkie ranked as a town of no small
importance. Centre of the See of Ross, it enjoyed a considerable
trade. Its market-cross — an octagonal sandstone slab with cap on
top, built into a square box of stones, five or six feet square and
about two feet high — graced the west end of the High Street,
whose centre was paved. Here extensive markets were held, and
merchants came from far and near to do business. On these
occasions six to ten "pretty men" were chosen as town guard, with
a duly elected captain. Everyone chosen was "under payne of
fyne" if he did not accept.

A circular mound existed on the terrace above the town,
towards the West End. This was known as Court Hill, and here,
and at Gallow-bank, justice was dispensed with no light hand, for
Rosemarkie's bailies had great
power and privilege. There was
a food controller, and fines
were imposed on anyone found
polluting springs or wells. The
Tolbooth held a sinister threat
over and above imprisonment,
for its key was made red-hot,
and used to brand the left cheek
of any culprit convicted of
theft. The Sabbath Day was
rigorously observed.

Yet, over the latter part of
this period, Rosemarkie was

slowly sealing its own doom. About 1227 the burghers felt the town must have more breathing-space, especially for its church buildings. A suitable site was selected about a mile away, at the Chanonry of Ros, and between 1227 and 1249 the See was gradually transferred there. The building done during these years continued up to about 1507 and ended triumphantly with a cathedral — one of the finest in Scotland — several canonries and church offices, and a magnificent bishop's palace.

So, in its turn, Fortrose gathered to itself a new life. In 1590 King James VI created Fortrose a royal burgh, with weekly markets and two yearly fairs. In 1592 he confirmed the union of Fortrose and Rosemarkie and all privileges granted to it by his predecessors, but now the united burgh was to be governed by the provost and council of Fortrose.

From now on the fortunes of Rosemarkie steadily declined. Sixty years later it was to be described as totally decayed, houses and buildings completely ruinous, if not demolished; the town itself depopulated except for a few poor fishermen; the haunt of stray delinquents and shiftless vagrants.

Meanwhile Fortrose prospered. Oliver Cromwell had marched north, and with puritanical zeal demolished part of the Cathedral-tower, nave, choir, and Lady Chapel — to provide stone for the building of his fort at Inverness. Fortrose survived even this blow, and a chronicler was still able to describe it in glowing terms as "a town of a most pleasant situation, whose population is increasing daily, and prospering in trade, politics and industries". At this time — in 1661 — the name of the united burgh was changed from Rosemarkie to Fortrose.

Before the destruction of its Cathedral Fortrose must have had a very beautiful and imposing appearance — somewhat like an English ecclesiastical town. It was naturally sunny, and the lands around it rich and in good order. The secluded Cathedral Green was surrounded by large old trees, the houses of the town, except for the twenty-two manses of the canons and presbyters, whose gardens and courtyards found entrance to it by Gothic arched gateways, being built at some distance from it.

An improvement in the affairs of Rosemarkie now began, stimulated, ironically enough, by association with its more prosperous neighbour. Fortrose, however, had not seen the last of its troubles. By 1686 it became clear to the bishop and his chapter that the difficulties of Episcopacy were likely to increase rather than diminish, and accordingly certain assets, including the grass of the cathedral green and some feus and duties were made over to the parish schoolmaster.

The first Presbyterian pastor was established about 1710 and from then onwards the ecclesiastical buildings fell into disuse. An observer of 1850 wrote sadly of Fortrose:

"Most of its ancient glory is now faded; its castle is razed to the ground; the bishop's palace and the residences of other dignitaries share the same fate; even its once grand cathedral presents but a fragment to convey to the inquirer a glimpse of its past grandeur; yet one feels the sanctity of its antique atmosphere while walking round the cathedral square, and very little imagination will conjure up the procession of surpliced priests and choristers".

Ruins and ghosts! That was all that remained of a cathedral which had been so important that it had practically acquired the status of a seat of government in the North.

Nevertheless, a wonderfully robust town grew up amidst the crumbling treasures of Fortrose's past — a town whose gracious buildings retained the quiet dignity of the old burgh. Even today the beautiful structure of what remains of the Cathedral still dominates the plan, and the many residences which were connected with it lend distinction to its streets.

The present High Street runs, more or less, in front of where the abodes of the chief church officials stood. Castle Street was the locus of several manses. Academy Street housed the Archdean and Archdeacon, whilst in Flowerburn Lodge grounds was the Bishop's Palace. The Deanery, with its quaint Roman arch still flanks the south side of Rose Street — the main building being known as Angel Court.

The closing down of the passenger service to Fortrose seemed to toll its death knell. By now the town had become, like Rosemarkie, a rather delightful seaside resort, known to few outside the Highlands. It could offer a good nine hole golf course, and excellent trout and sea fishing.

The pattern of Rosemarkie's well-being was also now clearly defined. Its long stretch of beach had become its most important feature. Today it terminates a row of fine houses fringing the Bay, with the bright pink surface of tennis courts to give colour to the scene. To the rear, however, there still runs a veritable maze of short narrow roads and alleys, witness of the busy and congested life of its earlier years.

The wheel continued to spin. A new invention, altering the way of society in the shape of the television transmitter for the Highland Area, brought its magic to almost forgotten Rosemarkie. Once more this little burgh basked in the limelight.

Chapter 8

Tales of Badenoch

NO part of Scotland is richer in legend and tradition than Speyside. This countryside of dark, dense forests, lofty hills and turbulent rivers, provides a fitting background for the macabre and the supernatural.

At one time the glens and moors of Badenoch, from Glentruim to Glenfeshie, were a vast forest of oak and fir, forming part of the hunting domain of that ferocious baron, the Red Comyn. The few pockets of land under cultivation were confined to the dells by the waterside — the rearing of flocks being much more popular than the cultivation of land.

On a spot known as The Craig, overlooking the main entrance to Glentromie, and a little to the east of the shooting lodge, cut out of the face of a rock, is Farquhar's Chair. Big Farquhar, a giant over eight feet in height, was at one time the farmer of Invertromie — a man whose stout cudgel could fell ten assailants at a blow. He had one son, who, disdaining a farmer's life, joined a band of freebooters in Lochaber.

About this time Farquhar's wife left him and went to live with Donald Dhu, a widower with nine sons, whose home was at Glentromie. Farquhar, piqued, made up his mind to find himself another companion, and did, in the person of Grace, one of the ladies of the Red Comyn's court. The Red Comyn was furious, and had the two immediately brought before him. Realising that both were determined on their new venture, he gave Big Farquhar the choice of marrying the lady, or being hanged.

Big Farquhar naturally chose the lesser evil and agreed to marry Grace. Now her brother was Comyn's chief henchman — so through his marriage Big Farquhar gained favour at the court. After a while, however, Farquhar's fortunes began to decline. Some of the animals mysteriously disappeared. Keeping watch one dark night for the marauders, he caught and killed three of them — and then was horrified to find that he had despatched three members of Red Comyn's court. A message from Grace's brother warned him to flee from the district for his life.

The bold Farquhar fled to Donald Dhu's house in Glentromie, and there waxed fat and happy in the care of his first wife — sunning himself in the stone armchair which he himself had fashioned out of the rock. This was more than Donald Dhu could stand. He summoned his nine sons and they agreed to kill Big Farquhar. This they did while he dozed in his armchair.

Unknown to them, their activities had been watched by a pedlar who had often passed the time of day with Big Farquhar, and he lost no time in telling Farquhar's son what had happened. The latter, helped by his mother, gained entrance to Donald Dhu's house and killed him and all his nine sons, cutting off their heads and piling them on top of a hillock, near the wayside between the farmhouse of Killiehuntly and Glentromie shooting lodge. The hillock is still known at Ceann na Torr — "The Head of the Hillock." Gathering all the cattle and goods he could find, and taking his mother with him, he escaped with his spoil to his retreat in Lochaber.

Near Kingussie, in a croft known as Bean-an-Lagain, dwelt a famous witch, whose continual depredations on the stocks of the neighbouring crofters forced them to take resolute action. Finding the witch's sheep eating his corn, one crofter enclosed them and demanded payment for the damage done. The witch had to pay up, but vowed a terrible revenge on the unfortunate crofter, who immediately fell sick and died. Next his barn was burnt down, and his house haunted by a ferocious black cat. So horrified did his widow become that she and her family left the district.

Some time afterwards a new shepherd, Donald Bane, took over the croft — and to ward off the Evil One, had a sprig of bog myrtle tied to the horns and tail of each cow; the byre protected by rowan branches, the house by a horseshoe nailed on the door. Even so, he could not get rid of the black cat — and chickens and eggs continued to disappear. Suspecting the black cat to be none other than the witch, Donald put a silver button in his gun and fired at the brute, hitting it on one of its hind legs. It uttered a blood-curdling scream and disappeared — but the next time the witch was seen, she walked with a limp.

Shortly after this Donald went to stay at the bothy at Corrour. One wet day he was sitting at his fireside, drying his clothes, when a black hen appeared beside him. The dogs growled. Donald blessed himself in fear and trembling. As he watched, the hen grew bigger — and suddenly changed into the witch.

"Tie up your dogs!" she commanded.

"I have nothing with which to tie them," answered Donald.

"Take these," she hissed, taking a few rough hairs from her head.

Donald put the hairs on the sleeve of his wet coat, and immediately the witch sprang on him like a tigress.

"Tighten hairs, cut and strangle," screamed the witch, as she lunged at him — but the dogs proved too fierce for her, and as she fled, chased her along the road.

Next morning Donald was out at dawn. Near the bothy he found one of his dogs dead — a piece of human flesh in its mouth. When he arrived home he was told that the witch was dead.

Her body was carried to a small hillock, where it was burned. A hole on the top of this mound marks the place. When this hillock was planted with trees, none could be made to take root on this spot.

The name Dalwhinnie is a corruption of a Gaelic term meaning "The Dell of Meeting" — and, in olden times, it was here that Highland chiefs and barons of the South met to iron out their differences. Often these meetings ended in bloodshed, to which the many graves, half-hidden in the heather, still bear witness.

On one occasion a meeting was arranged between Lochiel and Atholl. Lochiel, not altogether trusting Atholl, felt he had better consult the prophetess of the district before undertaking the journey. Her advice to him was, "Trust not yourself unarmed near Atholl. He intends to kill you."

"But he has arranged to meet me, bringing only two attendants, and I have agreed to go on the same footing," rejoined Lochiel.

"Be warned, sire," the prophetess insisted. "Trust not yourself near Dalwhinnie without a strong body of your clan or you shall never see Lochaber again."

Fearful of treachery, Lochiel ordered two hundred of his clan to hide in the hills near Dalwhinnie, ready to attack if necessity arose.

As arranged, Atholl, with two attendants, was waiting when he arrived, and greeted him in a most friendly manner before beginning to discuss affairs. Lochiel's conscience began to prick. He should not have distrusted Atholl. What if any of his followers were detected before the meeting ended?

Atholl was wearing a short, grey cloak lined with red, which kept slipping off as they talked. Suddenly, as if by accident, he turned it inside out before replacing it on his shoulders. As if by magic, heads of Atholl clansmen appeared along the hillside.

"Who are these?" demanded Lochiel.

"Only Atholl sheep coming to eat Lochaber grass," sneered Atholl.

Lochiel stood up and waved his bonnet.

Immediately the surrounding hills were covered by his men.

"What have we here?" shouted Atholl.

"Only Lochaber dogs ready to worry Atholl sheep. Draw, traitor, and defend your life."

A bloody conflict ensued in which the Camerons were the victors — and to this day the graves of the Atholl clansmen can be seen a little to the west of Dalwhinnie.

Before the old wooden bridge was built at Ruthven, the only means of crossing the Spey near Kingussie was either to ford the river — an adventure which often proved dangerous — or to pay for a crossing by boat. In the olden days the Kingussie boathouse stood in the hollow — somewhat nearer to the village than the present bridge. The boatman was a person of some importance. He had a house and garden beside the ferry — and was expected to hold himself in readiness for a crossing from either side at any hour. The fare for his service was one penny.

One year during the celebration of Communion at Kingussie the Spey was in flood, and the people were forced to cross by boat. The boatman at this time was a greedy, unprincipled wretch, who, taking advantage of the situation, demanded sixpence from his fares — without giving them warning of the change of price. His ultimatum was "no sixpence, no crossing."

In consequence of this, several people were deterred from attending Communion — amongst them being a pious old woman over ninety years of age, who had attended regulary for over fifty years. In vain she pleaded with the boatman, promising to pay the balance of the money at a later date. Heavy in heart, she was forced to return home.

The ministers and elders missed her well-known face from the congregation, and a few days later one of the elders called at her cottage to find out why she had not attended the service. He found her confined to bed, and near her end. She told him what had happened. The elder immediately sought out the boatman, and conveyed to him the prediction made by the old woman: "You

cruelly refused to bring a poor woman across the water, where she
wished to come for the purpose of attending the sacrament of our
Lord, because she had not enough money to satisfy your greedy
soul. For this, vengeance will overtake you here and hereafter.
Here you will be deprived of your living, as well as of your house
and land; you will die an unnatural death, and your body will be
devoured by beasts."

How true the prediction proved to be! About a year later a
wooden bridge was erected across the Spey at Ruthven — and no
boatman then being required, the tyrant was forced to earn a
scanty living in the village, doing any odd job that came to hand.

At that time a corn mill stood on the site occupied by Granite
House, in the High Street. It was destroyed by fire in the first half
of the 20th century. The miller employed the boatman occasionally to clean out pigsties and do odd jobs about the mill. One day the
miller told him to turn the water off the mill. To do this he had to
walk along a narrow plank which ran from the upper loft to the
sluice.

The water was duly turned off, but no boatman returned to the
mill! Some time later the miller found the pigs devouring his body.
He had slipped from the plank on his way back to the mill, and
fallen into the sty which was directly underneath.

It was only in the vicinity of strong castles that people knew
safety, and even then, only so long as they remained loyal to their
masters. Sometimes these lords proved cruel — and one of the
most vicious and debauched was one of the Comyns, the Black
Comyn, son of the first Lord Badenoch. A descendant of his,
known as Red Comyn, was killed at Dumfries by Robert Bruce.

At Ruthven Castle the seneschal of the Black Comyn was
Muriach Ruadh (Red Murdoch), a petty tyrant of the worst type.
Old and young dreaded the sight of Murdoch, avoiding him as
much as possible.

One fine morning, about the end of August, Murdoch sallied
forth from the castle with an armed guard and trumpeters. The
frightened tenants ran to their homes and hid. On reaching the
centre of the village the party halted and the trumpeters blew a
loud blast. Red Murdoch stepped forward and delivered his
message, which was that all females between the ages of twelve and
thirty years were required to shear the baron's corn on the third
day following, and were to do this in a state of nudity.

Consternation gripped the people — but they dared not hope to defy the command, for they knew what they might expect from their ruthless overlord if they did — certain death. One very pretty young woman had reason to dread the shearing day more than the others, for Red Murdoch had already cast lecherous eyes upon her. She appealed to her sweetheart, a young man whose grandmother was reputed to be a witch — and on her advice he appeased her worries, saying, "Have no fears, neither Black Comyn nor Red Murdoch will live to see the day."

With some boon companions, the Black Comyn was to ride across the hills from Blair Atholl, to be met on the way by Red Murdoch and his band. On the morning before shearing day, Murdoch and his party left the castle as arranged and kept a rendezvous with his master. None of them was ever seen alive again. At dusk a horse cantered to the gate of Ruthven Castle bearing on its saddle part of the mangled body of Red Murdoch. In a narrow valley in the wilds of Gaick, fragments of clothes and dismembered bodies told the tale of a deadly struggle in which Comyn and his entire party had been killed. The place is still called "The Pass of the Comyns."

What had happened? There may have been a natural enough explanation, but if so it is not known to locals.

About the year 1532 the then Cluny MacPherson arranged to marry his eldest daughter to one of the great chiefs of Ulster. The chief duly arrived from Ireland with his retinue of warriors to celebrate the wedding. During the festival one of his retinue, Cathalan, fell in love with the bride's younger sister. Cluny however, would never agree to his daughter's marriage with anyone who was not a clan chief, so the lovers decided to elope.

Finding the time of year inopportune for this adventure, however, Cathalan returned to Ireland with the Lord of Ulster. In the fall of the year, along with a faithful servant, he returned to Badenoch and lost no time in getting in touch with his sweetheart. Together they fled.

Their plan was to cross over the pass of Corrieyairack and then, by journeying down the West Coast, eventually to cross to Ireland by boat. They travelled about seven miles of very difficult road up the glen, and then the lady's strength gave out. Footsore and weary, she found she could go no farther. Night was coming on, so they sought refuge in a solitary cave, known to this day as "Creag-a-Cathalain".

The old chief, alarmed at his daughter's absence, soon

discovered what had taken place. Summoning his gillies, he sent
them in pursuit of the lovers — swearing that nothing but the heart
of the Irishman would appease his anger — and forbade them to
return, under penalty of death, without it.

It did not take long for the gillies to find the direction the lovers
had taken, and almost immediately the hunt was on. Early in the
morning of the following day the lovers left the cave and began to
travel towards Corrieyairack. Unfortunately for them, snow had
fallen overnight and lay like a white sheet over mountain and glen.
Their pursuers found it easy to trace their footprints and overtook
them about two miles beyond the cave.

Surrounded by enemies, Cathalan put up a desperate fight, but
in the end was overcome by Cluny's men who murdered him, cut
out his heart as instructed, and took it back to Cluny.

From some papers found in the dead man's wallet, Cluny was
surprised to find that he had been a person of much higher
integrity in his own country than Cluny had imagined him to be.
He made up his mind to acknowledge this fact, which suited his
Highland pride — for he could now claim that it was no mere
"duine usual" or bonnet laird who had carried off his daughter,
but a rightful thane of Ulster.

The old chief later expressed his sorrow for having, in his anger,
ordered the death of Cathalan — and to mark his regret publicly,
had a standing stone placed over his grave. The stone, a fragment
of which still remains, must at that time have been a very
conspicuous landmark in this lonely district, standing as it did on a
level part of the wild glen.

What became of the young lady is not known. Cathalan's trusty
servant, sent on ahead to arrange about the boat, eventually got
back to Ireland and never returned to Badenoch. The broken
stone in the quiet glen is all that remains to remind one of the tragic
tale of the terrible vengeance of Cluny.

About the end of the 18th century a wayside inn kept by a
widow, Bell Fraser, stood on the old drove road, about half a mile
north-east of Loch Gynack. Along this road were small, cultivated
patches, with a few goats and sheep, but there were also fertile
acres with herds of cattle and large flocks of sheep. Bell Fraser
owned one of these richer holdings at a place called Braecherach.

During the summer months crofters sent their cattle to graze on
the hills, in charge of herds. On one occasion the Braecherach
cattle strayed on to the land of Mackintosh of Borlum, who owned

what is known today as the Balavil Estate. Seeing the cattle encroaching on his land, Borlum proceeded to drive them farther on to it.

The herds, Duncan Fraser, aged fourteen, son of widow Fraser, and Maggie Mackintosh, aged twelve, daughter of the innkeeper at Tigh-na-Camahe, alarmed, ran to rescue them. Borlum, furious, seized the boy and began to beat him mercilessly.

Travelling with his attendants to Edinburgh at this time was Sir Hector Munro of Novar. Hearing the screams of the children, he cantered across to see what was wrong. Horrified, he shouted to Borlum to stop hitting the boy, and, jumping from his horse, led the lad away, warning him to keep his cattle off Borlum's land in the future.

About a year later Maggie was at home when one of Borlum's servants called to see her eldest brother. Being a Mackintosh, Borlum could demand his services whenever he chose. As she listened, unnoticed, Maggie heard the name of Novar mentioned, and to her horror learned that a plan was afoot to attack and rob Sir Hector when he crossed the River Dulnain on his next journey to Edinburgh.

She immediately thought of Duncan and ran to his home. Here she told him and his mother what she had overheard. They made up their minds to try to find out when Novar would be passing and warn him of his danger. They had not long to wait. Next night a drover arrived at the inn from the South, and in conversation with other guests remarked, "I would not be here tonight were it not that Novar's men have taken up all the beds in Dalwhinnie."

Immediately Duncan heard this he set out for Dalwhinnie, and arriving there early next morning, warned Novar of his danger. At first Sir Hector refused to believe him.

"Why have you come to warn me?" he asked. "Who are you?"

"I am the herd boy Borlum was thrashing when you came along and stopped him."

"Ah, I remember", Novar answered. "You are a good lad, and I will not forget what you have done." He sat down and wrote a letter. This he gave to Duncan along with a guinea, charging him to deliver the letter at once to the officer at Ruthven Barracks.

Duncan lost no time in getting to Ruthven. That evening a party of soldiers left the barracks there and joined Novar and his retinue. As they prepared to cross the River Dulnain in the late evening they were immediately attacked by Borlum and his men.

A desperate fight ensued, with heavy losses on both sides. Mackintosh of Borlum escaped, but his natural brother was seized, tried at Inverness and hanged. Borlum was proclaimed an outlaw, his estates being confiscated by the Crown. These were eventually bought by James MacPherson of Ossian fame.

True to his promise, Novar took Duncan into his service. A few years later Duncan and Maggie married and their descendants were living near Culloden about 1875.

Chapter 9

From Norse Haven to Millionaire's Castle

THE country bordering the north side of the Dornoch Firth has an unspoiled beauty and an air of withdrawn-ness from the busy world that never fails to charm me. Visitors hurrying to the more rugged attractions of the North-West too often remain unaware of what lies to the east of Bonar Bridge. It is a countryside of woods and great sea views and of villages which speak of a long acquaintance with ordered ways. Dornoch is the biggest centre of population, but Skibo with its castle, famous as the home of Andrew Carnegie, is perhaps the best point from which to look around.

Skibo, in modern times the home and pleasure gardens of millionaires, has attracted settlers from earliest days. Over seven hundred years ago this secluded spot was known to the Norse by the name of Scithaboll or Schythebolle. "Skeith" was the Norse term for "ship of war", and "bol" indicated a farm or cultivated land. From the Dornoch Firth a narrow bay runs up to the land immediately in front of Skibo Castle — giving Skibo its own private stretch of sailing water. Into this haven the Norse reivers steered their galleys, and impressed by the fertility of the land around, chose it as a permanent place of residence. Here they built a fort and other buildings which they surrounded with a high rampart. Thus the beginnings of what we now know as Skibo were laid.

In the early thirteenth century, Skibo attracted the attention of a very different type of person, and was for a period, the summer residence of Bishop Gilbert and other Church dignitaries of the See of Sutherland and Caithness. The beauty and abundance of its gardens and orchards became celebrated.

The then Earl of Sutherland cast covetous eyes on Skibo and when Bishop Archibald succeeded to the See in 1275, a long drawn-out quarrel took place between the two. This was finally resolved in favour of the Church and the castle became thenceforth, the principal residence of the Bishops of the diocese.

There was one Bishop, however, who failed to respond to Skibo's charms. He was Bishop Robert Stewart, brother of the Earl of Lennox. Finding worldly affairs more exciting than the business of his See, he lived for long periods in the South of Scotland and England, becoming deeply involved in the intrigues of the courts of England and France, and the many quarrels amongst the nobles during Mary's minority and the regency of her mother.

In 1650 Montrose was confined in Skibo for several days after his capture in Assynt. A century later the estate was in the possession of the Hon. George MacKay, half-brother to Lord Reay, who was responsible for the planting of the older portion of its beautiful woods. In 1786 Skibo was purchased by George Dempster of Dunnichen, grandson of a Dundee merchant, who, being an eminent agriculturist, threw himself heart and soul into the task of making Skibo the realisation of his dreams. The estate remained in the Dempster family for about eighty years, and the memory of the good deeds and unselfish life of George Dempster was long cherished.

Indulgent to their servants and tenantry, and devoted to their home, the Dempsters perfected what generations of loving proprietors had laboured to create.

The estate passed, in the year 1866, to an Australian named Chernside and six years later it was bought by Evan Sutherland Walker for £130,000. Mr Walker greatly improved the castle and outbuildings, and at the end of his ownership the former home of the Norse reivers had developed into an estate of some 20,000 acres, boasting a handsome castle, and grounds and policies which could not be surpassed in beauty anywhere in the county.

But Skibo's most famous owner was of course Andrew Carnegie. One might well ask what strange chance brought the steel millionaire to Skibo and why, in 1897 he decided to make his home there. Andrew Carnegie

was very much his mother's son — a mother whom he admiringly invariably referred to as "The Queen Dowager". Margaret Morrison came of an interesting line of Celts. Her father, Thomas Morrison, was the champion of the "Charter of Liberty" in Dunfermline, and being a naturally eloquent orator often preached in The Tabernacle in Leith Walk, Edinburgh. Andrew Carnegie inherited much of the Celtic spirit and tastes of his mother's family.

Yet another relative, a maternal uncle, Mr George Lauder, inspired in him passion for natural beauty. Lauder's readings of Burns' poems made an abiding impression on young Carnegie and when the boy left the school where he received his brief education, he, too, was able to recite almost every known work of Burns, and, in addition, many lovely old Scottish poems and ballads. His power of memorising poetry remained an outstanding characteristic all his life — and it was from Burns that he adopted his maxim for living, when only twenty-one years of age — "Thine own reproach alone do fear". This quotation, which he carried everywhere with him, and eventually hung on his library wall in Skibo Castle, was his guide and counsellor throughout his busy life.

Carnegie extended the estate to include the River Shin, one of the best angling rivers in Scotland. At Skibo, he and his wife, the former Miss Louise Whitfield, of New York, entertained extensively, including among their guests, society personalities, leading politicians and literary figures of that era.

Skibo is an ideal possession. An unusual feature is the variety of pleasure walks. There are a laburnum walk, where laburnums flourish over an undergrowth carpeted with blue hyacinths; a lilac walk, where mauve and white lilacs nod over anemones and primroses; gay rhododendron walks fringed by azaleas; the secluded monks' walk, cloistered by tall elms which arch overhead, seeming for all the world like the stately pillars and pointed arches of some ancient cathedral; the terrace walk where trees, planted by eminent visitors invite our inspection — each bearing a plate with the name of the person who planted it, and the date of planting; scented rose walks; and the rugged natural walk to the bay — meandering past huge hothouses, with their peaches and nectarines, past the marble-floored swimming pool, down the wooded glade to the water's edge, where, on call, lives the boatman to row one across the Meikle Ferry.

Although Andrew Carnegie is dead, one is always conscious of his influence. At Skibo all was organised and used to benefit owner and servant alike. It was as if Andrew Carnegie had never forgotten those dreary months spent in a bobbin factory in Pittsburg, where, for the miserly sum of three shillings per week he was forced to squander his health and stamina. His workers must have a square deal. They, too, must enjoy Skibo!

It was his custom to go the round of his servant's houses on Sunday morning after church — inquiring whether the various families had attended divine worship, or whether they might have "slipped" owing to Saturday night conviviality. Needless to say, the Highlander enjoyed his Saturday night's dram, and often hurried off to the kirk with his family on the Sunday morning, leaving a tell-tale bottle on the parlour table. It was on such occasions that many an elderly granny shook Carnegie warmly by the hand, with the bottle hastily hid behind the cushion of her armchair, and accepted his golden sovereign, the usual reward for a tidy house and good behaviour.

Andrew Carnegie was married in 1887 and his daughter, Margaret, was not born until 1897, the year he came to Skibo. One can imagine the joy with which this event was heralded, and how Skibo came to mean "Home" to the Carnegie family, in a way that no other place had ever done. To the descendants of Margaret it is still home, and ever will be, in spite of the sorrow sustained by them a few years ago, when Margaret's daughter, happy mother of five young children, died there after a few days' illness, from polio.

Five miles from Skibo lies Dornoch. In the past the *raison d'etre* for Dornoch was religion. Today it is golf — though golf was played there as early as 1616, when Earl John, thirteenth Earl of Sutherland was being educated. These two interests have combined to produce a small town, rich in tradition, yet well equipped for modern living. Built on flat ground, it is well protected from the north winds by a high embankment, which shelters the magnificent golf course. The panorama of sea and country obtainable from almost every hole is remarkable.

The derivation of the name Dornoch has long been given incorrectly as "Dorneich", meaning "horse-hoof" — an error which had a strange repercussion. Tradition has it that in the thirteenth century a duel was fought between the Thane of Sutherland and a Norse leader, whom the Earl, having dropped his sword, slew with a horse's hoof, which lay near at hand. When Charles I declared Dornoch a Royal Burgh, the corporate body adopted a horseshoe, with the motto "Sans Peur", as the burghs arms.

When, however, a mandate of King David, drawn up about 1136 was later discovered, in which the town was named as Durnach, the derivation was shown to be fallacious. Durnaig or Dornaig, are obsolete Gaelic words for pebbles, and describe vividly the pebbly links, which have always been so important to the town. These, in the words of Sir Robert Gordon, writing of them in 1628, were "the fairest and largest links in Scotland, fit for archery, golfing, ryding and all other exercise".

The town itself still savours of its religious past. The cathedral, after being besieged and burned in 1570, was eventually rebuilt by the Duchess-Countess of Sutherland. It now has about a thousand sittings.

Two miles from Dornoch is the village of Clashmore, with its inviting inn. There is also the delightful fishing village of Embo, where once stood the old Castle of Embo, seat of the Gordons of that ilk. Near at hand is Skelbo, where on an eminence rising abruptly from the shore, stood a fortress, residence of a Norse nobleman.

A little west of Dornoch is Sitheraw, meaning the South Hall. Here, it is said, the redoubtable Siguard Eysteinson, who subdued Caithness and Sutherland, and defeated and killed Malbrigd of the "buck-tooth" in 875, was buried, and a great cairn raised over his grave. It was here, too, that the glass for the windows of Dornoch Cathedral was manufactured.

Lastly, I would mention the attractive village of Spinningdale, beautifully situated on the banks of the Kyle of Dornoch. In the early 1790s, a cotton manufactory was erected here employing more than a hundred hands from the district. The end of this industry was brought about in 1806, by a fire, which completely destroyed the building.

Here is a district small in area, but rich beyond its size in features of natural beauty.

Chapter 10

Why the Black Isle?

THE Black Isle of Ross-shire, that lovely and interesting tract of
country lying between the Cromarty and Beauly Firths, is apt
to lose appeal for the tourist on account of the forbidding vision
conjured up by its name. Yet, the moment we see "The Black Isle"
we are struck by two things — it is not black, and it is not an island.

Many years ago I asked a native about it. I drew his attention to
the fact that the place is not an island. It is a peninsula.

"But it is an island", he reiterated. "You have got the Cromarty
Firth on the north side, the Moray Firth on the east side, and the
Beauly Firth on the south side. In Gaelic the word 'Eilean'
meaning isle or island was made to include land partly or nearly
surrounded by water, as well as land wholly surrounded by water.
In Gaelic it's an island right enough". With this Gilbertian
explanation, I had, at the time, to be content.

Several years later, while pursuing the works of an old Highland minister, I stumbled across part of the correct explanation,
and at a later date learned the whole truth about this incongruous
name.

About the year 990 A.D. there was born in the town of Tain one
who afterwards became patron saint of that town — St Duth or
Duthac. The parents of St Duthac were of high rank.

Duthac was a prodigy of piety from his earliest years — so much
so that he was venerated by the country people even as a boy. He
finished his education in Ireland, and so fine a reputation did he
gain that he eventually became the Chief Confessor of Ireland and
Scotland. Later he returned to Tain, where he became the head of
a missionary band that preached the Gospel throughout Ross-
shire, particularly in Easter Ross and the so-called Black Isle. He
died at Armagh, Ireland in 1065.

The Gaelic name for Tain is "Baile Dhuthaich", the town of
Duthac, and such was the veneration of the good people of Tain
for their saint that on the 19th June 1253, nearly two hundred

years after his death and burial, they had his dust "translated" from Armagh to Tain, and buried in the sacred place that is still known as the Shrine of St Duthac.

Yet, though St Duthac primarily belongs to Tain, there is ample evidence from place names in the Black Isle that he journeyed extensively in that district. Let us examine a few of these:—

(1) Belmaduthy. This is a favourite seat of the Kilcoy family, and is situated about the centre of the Black Isle. The Gaelic name for this place is Bail-Mag-Dhuith, meaning "the town of the rig of Duthac". From this it is clear that here a rig or croft of land had been gifted to St Duthac. There is a sacred well near Belmaduthy mansion-house, from which, according to tradition, the saint used to drink, and this well was visited even by kings when on their pilgrimages to the holy shrine of St Duthac. Above Belmaduthy is a placed called Braemacatie. The Gaelic for this is Braighmag-duith, "the upper end of Duthac's rig or croft".

(2) Suddie. This is the name of a small estate south of Belma-duthy, and means simply "the see or seat of Duthac".

(3) Cnoc-Gille-Chuir-Duith, which means "the hill of the servant that Duthac sent". This hill is of a rounded form, and has got a sacred well to which offerings were made on its north-east side. It is thought that Duthac, when preaching elsewhere, sent a servant to officiate here in his stead, and the side of this hill was the platform from which he addressed his congregation.

(4) Tradition tells us that the old name of Drumderfit, situated about a mile south of Munlochy, was Drumdu or Drumduie, meaning "the Ridge of Duthac".

(5) Drynie, a small estate near Drum-derfit, is, in Gaelic, spelt Droighean-Dhuith, and means "the briar bush of Duthac". At Drynie there is a well, sacred to Duth or Duthac. Nearby grew a briar bush, on which the people placed rags as offerings to their saint. Glaic-An-Duthaig was a pretty hollow on the estate of Drynie, which was a favourite retreat of St Duthac. Translated literally this means "the hollow of our Duthac".

(6) Culbokie, situated in the parish of

Ferintosh. This name, when understood, conjures up a picture in our imagination of the life of the saint. The Gaelic name for Culbokie is Cul-Bhacaidh — a word made up of four words jumbled together — Cul-Bha-Aig-Duith, meaning "the small back closet that Duthac had". From this it is evident that Duthac was the great original evangelist of Ferintosh, and was the first to preach the Gospel of Christ there. Each day, after his labours, a small back room somewhere in Culbokie served as his place for sleep, meditation and prayer.

(7) The Gaelic name for Muir of Ord is Blar-Dubh or Duth, meaning Muir of Duthac.

(8) Avoch. The old name for Avoch was Achie, or Ach Dhuith, meaning the field of Duth or Duthac. A field was gifted to Duthac near the present village of Avoch, and this field gave Avoch — pronounced Auch — its name.

(9) The old name for Rosehaugh was Pittonnachie, meaning "the town of John of the field of Duthac". John was an assistant or missionary of St Duthac, who, in course of time, acquired the lands from this very circumstance, Pittonnachie.

(10) Killen. The Gaelic for Killen is Cill-Ean-Dhuith, meaning "the Cell of John (the servant) of Duthac".

These are only a few of many examples which may be quoted to show how the name of Duth or Duthac crops up in the names of places in the Black Isle, or "Eilean Dubh". Now "th" and "bh" are pronounced alike in Gaelic — so we have the terms "Eilean Dubh" and "Eilean Duth" sounding exactly the same. The explanation leaps at one — the correct term being "Eilean Duth", meaning "The Island of Duth or Duthac". On realising this, the repugnant epithet "Black" recedes from our minds.

For some years I thought of the Black Isle as St Duthac's Isle. Then one day I learnt something else. To the east of Borgie, in the parish of Tongue, there is a greensward with the remains of a ruined house thereon, which tradition says was given by the King of Scotland to Farquhar Beaton, the famous physician, who built a hunting lodge there. Some of the natives call this place Allan Nan Gall, others Eilean Nan Gall. It is an inland meadow, with no water near it.

A native again supplied the information. "It should be Allan — a form of the Gaelic Ailean", he said, "meaning a meadow". Eilean is just wrong. That's all!"

Thus the whole truth became clear at last. Eilean Dubh should have been Allan Duth, meaning St Duthac's Meadow.

Criticism to this solution of a long standing mystery has been offered on the point that Black Isle and Eilean Duth are comparatively modern names. In the old maps it was known as Ardmaunach. Consideration of this only strengthens our case.

St Duthac, as already stated, died in Armagh in 1065. A quotation from the old Irish annals runs: "1065 A.D. Duthach Albanach Praecipuus Confessarious Hiberniae Et Alban, in Ardmacha Quievit", which translated reads, "Duthac of Alban, the chief confessor of Ireland and Scotland, died in Armagh, in A.D. 1065". St Duthac's dust was "translated" to Tain in 1253.

When written about in Latin, he was elegantly called Ardmanachensis, for Ardmachanensis, which latter was not considered good Latin. Thus Allanduth was rendered, by the learned and ruling classes, as Ardmaunach. The common people, however, continued to call it "Allan-Duth", which when the memory of the Saint faded away, was corrupted into "Eilean Duth".

Beautiful peninsula — how right to name you Allanduth — the meadow of St Duthac — with your smiling green fields, your mild climate, and your calm, almost hushed way of life! Let us gaze on you and give praise for the beauty of the Creator's hand, the invention of His imagery, and the faith of one of His most devoted servants.

Chapter 11

A Castle Built to "Keep Up with the Joneses"

PLANES, buses, people — all the bustle and activity of an airport. How different from the original Dalcross! From their airport, eight miles east of the town, Inverness folk can be in London in less than two hours. Dalcross has seen some strange turns of history, but perhaps none more exciting than this.

The name Dalcross or Delginross meant Prickly Point or Prickly Wood, where whins or thorns grew in profusion. About 1330 we find Delginross described as a vicarage, depending on the Priory of Urquhart, and a modest agriculture was the only form of industry.

About 1500, Thomas, fourth Lord Fraser of Lovat, purchased the estate of Dalcross from Alexander Paterson — a prominent burgess of Inverness, and thus Dalcross became Lovat property.

In 1619 the ninth Lord Lovat, to please his second wife, who was a daughter of Lord James Stuart of Doune, agreed to build a castle at Dalcross. This Lady Lovat was cousin to the then Earl of Moray, who was at that time engaged in building Castle Stuart. "Keeping up with the Joneses" seems to have been the vogue even in these days, for it is recorded that it was this urge which impelled the lady to desire ownership of as good a castle as her cousin's, if not a better one, built near his, so that she might shine alongside her powerful relative.

Simon, Lord Lovat, falling in with the idea, set about the task with all speed, and decided to built not one, but two castles, the first at Dalcross and the second at Bunchrew.

The original Dalcross Castle, which lay about two miles northeast of Culloden battlefield consisted of two towers, joined at right angles, the inner corner, where they met, being covered with a projecting turret, and large entrance gate. The dais — a portion of the floor of the great hall, raised above the rest, for the special use of the Lord of the Manor, his family and principal guests — had special features of interest and the roof of one of the guest bedrooms was adorned with the coats of arms of the most powerful families in the country; amongst them those of the Bruces and the Earls of Huntly, Marischal, and Stuart.

In 1622, however, the year after the building of all three castles, Dalcross, Bunchrew, and Stuart, was completed, fate suddenly shot off two malignant darts. Lady Lovat's eldest son, Sir Simon of Inverallochy, died at Dalcross Castle, and shortly afterwards, she herself died at Bunchrew Castle. After the death of his second wife Lord Lovat married for the third time Catherine Rose of Kilravock.

For the next hundred years, Dalcross Castle was an important homestead, though within that time it had several proprietors. In the hands of the Lovats it was an agreeable country house, when they travelled to and from Morayshire, and lordly entertainments were held within its walls.

It was not, however, without its share in the troubles of the civil wars. In 1646 Lord Lewis Gordon, an ally of Montrose, burned its great cornyard on the very day on which Lord Hugh Fraser (son of Simon), tenth Lord Lovat, was interred at Kirkhill, near Beauly, where the flames were clearly visible to the funeral procession.

Three years after Hugh, tenth Lord Lovat, succeeded to the estates, his wife died, and her death seems to have cast such a gloom over his life that he practically retired from all his activities, leaving the management of his estates to his brilliant eldest son, Simon, Master of Lovat. The untimely death of this young man, however, necessitated the succession of the second son, Hugh, as Master of Lovat, with Sir James Fraser of Brea — second son of the ninth Lord Lovat's second wife — as tutor.

Sir James Fraser of Brea (1610-1649) was a staunch Covenanter, and kept the Frasers on the side of Church and Parliament in the Civil War, holding Inverness and its castle against Montrose. The heads of the clan, finding war a costly business, borrowed money from Sir James, who obtained Dalcross Castle and estate in mortgage. Here an old Celtic prophecy — "To pledge Dalcross is to lose Dal-

cross" — was fulfilled, for though Sir James himself did not become the actual proprietor, he left Dalcross in its mortgaged condition as a marriage portion to his eldest daughter, Jean.

In the Cromwellian garrison at Inverness was an officer, Captain George Bateman, a man of considerable means, who married Jean Fraser of Brea. When Lord Hugh Fraser of Lovat found it necessary to journey to England, Bateman lent him the money for the occasion, and for this obligement Lord Lovat granted him Dalcross Castle, thereby squaring off both the mortgage and the loan.

Bateman and his wife had no family, and he eventually sold Dalcross Castle to James Roy Dunbar, a bailie of Inverness, and relative of Provost Alexander Dunbar, founder of Dunbar's Hospital, Inverness. In 1702, James Roy Dunbar sold the castle and estate to the Mackintosh of Mackintosh and both still are the property of the present descendants of that family.

The Mackintoshes do not seem to have lived much in Dalcross Castle. In the eighteenth century, two Mackintosh chiefs lay there in state, prior to their interment in Petty, and the castle evidently became uncongenial to its owners. Little by little the handsome old edifice fell into decay. For years it stood a mere shell, one of the few features of interest to visitors being the hole in its main door made by a shot from one of Cumberland's cannon when he was advancing on Culloden. It was at Dalcross that Cumberland's troops were mustered in battle array by his officers, before entering on their last conflict with Prince Charlie's army on the same ridge — a little to the westward.

A new span of life was granted to the castle when Major MacAndrew, a well-known Inverness citizen, leased the ruin from The Mackintosh, and during the years 1897-1898, with the help of an Inverness architect, Mr W.L. Carruthers, rebuilt it to its original plan and transformed it into a most comfortable residence.

Dalcross was now readily let to the MacKinnon of MacKinnon, and he and his family found it a most congenial abode. Much of the furniture they brought to its rooms possessed a real historic interest, for the Hon. Mrs MacKinnon was a daughter of Lord Hood of Avalon, Somerset, and she owned many family relics which recalled naval and political incidents in which both MacKinnons and Hoods had played noteworthy parts. The MacKinnons had fought and distinguished themselves at Waterloo, while several members of the Hood family had held positions of the highest rank in Lord Nelson's fleet.

On the 14th September 1914, at the Battle of the Aisne, Alexander Hood MacKinnon, younger, of MacKinnon, was killed, and some little time later Dalcross Castle had new tenants. These were Harold Fraser-Simson and his wife, to whom I am indebted for much of the following.

Harold Fraser-Simson, born in London in 1878, was the eldest son of Arthur Theodore Simson and Catherine Fraser of Reelig. It is interesting here to note that Catherine Fraser of Reelig was a Lovat Fraser — for all Reelig Frasers are descended from Hugh Fraser of Reelig, natural son of the fifth Lord Lovat — so once again a Lovat came to live in Dalcross Castle. Educated at Charterhouse and in France, he was trained for shipping, in spite of his own fervid desire to study music, and in shipping he was forced to remain until he had sufficiently established himself as a musician to make the change of profession.

Having been born a natural musician he never acquiesced in the role chosen for him by his family. Whenever possible he attended concerts and studied the classics — composing part-songs, waltzes and ballads in his spare time. These last were sung on concert platforms by well-known singers of the day, such as Ada Crossley and Harry Dearth, often accompanied by the composer.

It was, however, the stage that fascinated him, and to satisfy this love he ran various amateur operatic societies — probably writing his first operetta, "Bonita", for one of these. Granville Barker saw it, and later produced it professionally in London. It was not a financial success, although some of his best music went into it, but it is more than likely it was through this that he got his chance to write "The Maid of the Mountains".

Daly's theatre commissioned him and a librettist to write a musical play to follow "The Happy Day" and then the management suddenly got "cold feet" about producing a play by unknown writers. The theatre was in a very bad way at the time. They were able to pay off the librettist, but could not afford to pay off the composer as well. They, therefore, engaged Frederick Lonsdale to write a libretto, and asked the composer, not very hopefully, to do his best to write suitable music. Contrary to expectation the play was an enormous success. It put Daly's on its feet again, ran in London for years, with two or three companies on tour. This was, of course, "The Maid of the Mountains".

Other musical plays, written for Jose Collins, Phyllis Dare and
Evelyn Laye, followed in quick succession. These were "Southern
Maid", "Our Peg", "Head Over Heels", "Our Nell", "Street
Singer", and "Betty in Mayfair".

By this time American syncopated rhythm was capturing popular taste. Because of his great gift for composing simple straight-
forward melody, this was a musical departure which Fraser-
Simson thoroughly disliked and would not engage in. He wrote
instead two ballets — "Venetian Wedding" and "Nightingale and
the Rose". Both were produced in London, and starred Nemchi-
mova, Markova and Anton Dolin.

One of his best friends was A.A. Milne, and the following
anecdote, in which this friend features, depicts the extremely shy,
modest genius that was Harold Fraser-Simson.

It was lunch time at the Garrick Club, and the two men were
seated at a table in animated discussion. The subject was the
setting to music of some of A.A. Milne's poems which were then
appearing every week in "Punch", delightfully decorated by E.H.
Shepherd, and creating quite a furore. Milne was recounting how
several composers had written to him offering to set one or other of
the poems to music. Should he accept? Fraser-Simson warned
against such a step, explaining how it would prove a mistake to
allow odd poems to be set to music by different composers, and
advised his friend to choose one really good composer such as
Edward German, who had been so successful with his settings for
Kipling's children's songs, to do the lot.

A day or two later they again met at the club, and again the same
topic was discussed. "Would you do the job?" Milne asked, and as
Fraser-Simson beamed his assent Milne asked, "Why on earth did
you not suggest yourself last time we met?" "I wanted to you have
the best", was the quiet rejoinder.

The result of this was an extremely happy collaboration, in
which Fraser-Simson wrote music for sixty-three of A.A. Milne's
"Christopher Robin" poems, and also music for "The King's
Breakfast" which was produced at the Vaudeville Theatre.

He then wrote the music for "Toad of Toad Hall", the children's
play adapted by A.A. Milne from Kenneth Grahame's book "The
Wind in the Willows". This was, perhaps, one of the things he
enjoyed composing most of all, for the music, which fits the play so
exactly, came so easily — almost spontaneously. It all just seemed
to be there!

Mrs Fraser-Simson, who died very recently, was herself a writer, and it was her first book, "Footsteps in the Night", which brought the film cameras to Dalcross. In this novel some of the scenes were laid at Dalcross Castle and in the district round about, and a very lovely setting was provided for the film which enjoyed the quite inappropriate title of "A Honeymoon Adventure". Mr Fraser-Simson wrote the theme song for this. This gifted musician met an untimely death by accident in 1944.

Chapter 12

Bagpipes Across the World

IT surprises many people to learn that pipers play for the Pope in Rome as part of the usual Italian Christmas-time festivities. Deeming the bagpipe as peculiar to the Highlands, and by no means ancient, they find it difficult to associate the instrument with the occasion. When one makes any sort of study of the history of the bagpipes, however, the origin of the custom soon becomes clear.

These pipers travel from the mountains of Southern Italy and play in the street. They go about in pairs — one having only a sort of chanter, almost like an overgrown clarionet, while the other carries a full set of pipes, the bag of which is made from a sheepskin, in the natural state. The chanter and drones are altogether more squat and short than those of the Highland bagpipe, and the whole thing is carried much as one carries a baby — the drones not being borne on the shoulder. The sound of the music from these instruments is entirely individual, providing a kind of rustic Pan piper effect — slightly out of tune, perhaps, but by no means unattractive — mystical, rather, and savouring of the long ago.

Tradition tells that on the day of Christ's birth the shepherds who tended their flocks and saw the brilliant star, heralding as it did tidings of great joy, played their bagpipes in the cave at Bethlehem, to express their exultation on the birth of the Infant Saviour.

Some may feel that tradition errs somewhat by making a cave the birthplace of our Saviour — but one must remember that in the Gospel narrative there is no mention of a stable, which is, in truth, merely the creation of poets and painters. In Bethlehem, the principal building is the convent of Nativity, built at the suggestion of the Empress Helena in 326, and beneath the church of which there is a grotto, said to be the place where Christ was born — the manger (a marble trough) in which He was laid being there also.

This tradition could very well be truth. The bagpipe, far from being modern, is actually one of the oldest, if not *the* oldest, of all musical instruments. The earliest form of wind instrument was undoubtedly the simple reed, blown by the prehistoric shepherd, who used to pipe for the pleasure of his flocks and herds, maintaining that this music induced flocks to come together and feed with relish. In the course of years, the advantage of having two holes in the reed was discovered. Then four holes allowed of the use of the fingers of both hands, while six holes and eventually eight gave greater compass and range of sound.

Several sculptured figures of Egyptian shepherds show their instrument known as the Arghool as consisting of two pipes of unequal length, attached to each other — the short pipe the chanter, and the longer pipe the drone — and here we meet the drone for the first time. As the centuries passed, it was found that when the simple reed pipe was inserted into one end of a bladder, and a short mouthpiece likewise inserted in the opposite end, one could obtain a continuity of melody far surpassing that produced by the more or less staccato note of the reed pipe. This invention was called a "chorus" and was undoubtedly the earliest form of bagpipe.

Pipers are referred to in the Lutheran translation of Genesis (4th chapter, 21st verse) and in the third chapter of Daniel (Revised Version), where Nebuchadnezzar's band is described — so what could be more likely than that they would play on the occasion of the birth of Christ?

Ancient Egypt was one of the earliest nations to employ the bagpipe. Professor Garstang provided indisputable evidence when he discovered a Hittite slab, which he dated about B.C. 1000, on which is sculptured a bagpipe player. Today the modern Egyptian "zummarah" has a goatskin bag, into which the two pipes are inserted.

Other sculptures found at various places and times depict pipers in Assyria, Tarsus, Thebes, China, India and Persia — the last being the most interesting as far as we are concerned, for the scale of the Persion bagpipe has been found to be almost identical with that of the Highland bagpipe chanter. From all this it is evident that the bagpipe had its origin in the East, and is an extremely ancient instrument.

How did the bagpipe come to Scotland? From the East the bagpipe travelled over almost every country. Greece derived her musical culture from Egypt. Dr Burney provides a drawing of an ancient gem in which Apollo is represented as walking with a lyre in his hand and a bagpipe slung over his shoulder.

The Romans employed the bagpipe to rouse their armies when on the march, an idea borrowed by them from the Greeks who had borrowed it from the Egyptians. The Romans, too, often held bagpipe competitions; at these a *capistrum*, a kind of leathern headstock, encircling the cheeks, was usually worn to safeguard the player from overstraining himself in blowing!

There is a sculptured bronze at Richborough Castle, in Kent, representing a Roman soldier in full military order playing the bagpipe. Pennant, in his "Tour of Scotland", mentions this as proof that the Romans introduced the bagpipe into Britain. This is incorrect, for the Celts had introduced the instrument into Britain a full century before the time of Caesar.

A word of explanation just here. The term Celtic is generally understood to refer only to the inhabitants of the Scottish Highlands, Wales, Ireland and elsewhere. The truth is that before there was a Celt in these islands there were Celts in most corners of the then known world, the East included, and it is through some of these wandering tribes who travelled to Ireland from the Continent that the bagpipe came to Britain. We find evidence in support of this in an Irish saga of the seventh century, where there is an account of those who came to pay homage to King Cocaire the Great, in B.C. 35, among them "nine pipers from the fairy hills of Bregia".

The Romans did, however, do much to popularise the bagpipe in Britain, by using it to accompany their armies when on the march, during their invasion of Britain, about 78-85 A.D.

From this time onwards the bagpipes were held in high esteem in England. At the time of the Anglo-Saxon conquest 450-580, they were popular. The Anglo-Normans took them up eagerly, and at this period they were commonly used in England in connection with church services and outdoor religious services.

The King's Band of Music under Edward III included pipers requisitioned for this event. Chaucer describes his "Miller" as a performer on the bagpipes, and it was to the sound of this instrument that the pilgrims rode to Canterbury.

Under James II the bagpipe still had an honoured position in England, and it was not till the reign of George II that the English bagpipe ceased to be a popular instrument. Northumbria was the only part where a certain type of bagpipe, the bellows-pipe, found favour, and Northumbrian pipers are spoken of with respect even to this day.

It is to two Irish colonisations, one in A.D. 120 and the second about 506, that the bagpipe owes it adoption in Scotland, and especially in the Highlands.

Though records are sparse, we can assume that the pipes steadily consolidated their appeal. We know that in the twelfth century, Giraldus Cambrensis, a Welshman, whose real name was Gerald Barry, visited Scotland and records that he found the "chorus" there in common use. There was a King's Piper in Scotland in the middle of the fourteenth century. We learn from the old Exchequer Rolls that David II of Scotland authorised a payment to this piper in 1362. When did the pipers first lead the Highlanders in war? On written evidence, since the Battle of Harlaw (1411). George Buchanan, the historian, emphasises the fact.

Until 1500 the standard bagpipe of the country was a two-droned pipe, and though the three-droned pipe was favoured by some players it was not until 1700 to 1800 that this came into general usage.

We may ask why the bagpipe has come to be considered an instrument characteristic of the Highlands, and why its popularity has waxed here and waned elsewhere? Strangely

Northumbrian pipes, operated by bellows.

French Musette pipes.

Crimean Tatar pipes.

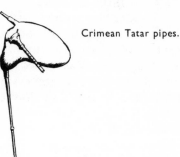

Early German pipes.

enough we find the answer to this in the Court of France. In the early thirteenth century the King's Piper at the Court of France was a famous French musician named Colin Muset. This man headed a school of pipers in that country which corresponded more or less to the MacCrimmon School at Boreraig — and sought to improve the instrument by converting it to a bellows-pipe. This new development was commended by many at the time — but the result was that eventually this bagpipe degenerated into an instrument of household music, finding its way into the salons of that and slightly later centuries.

To the Highlander this new instrument was an abomination. It did not suit his warlike spirit or his way of life. Other countries adopted the French form of pipe and shared in the eventual decline of pipe music, but the Highlander remained faithful to the old bagpipe, developing it and its music in accordance with his own ideas and requirements. It is the Highlander and no one else who merits the credit for the instrument as we know it today — the Highland bagpipe, proudly carried with the bag placed underneath the arm and the three drones, the largest carrying his banner, on the shoulder.

The adoption of the instrument for use with the British Army furthered its popularity both at home and abroad. This important event took place over three hundred years ago, when Britain's standing army was raised. The first world war accorded its impelling music a worldwide welcome, and today, "the skirl of the pipes" can be heard in almost every country in the world.

Chapter 13

Somerled MacDonald, Artist and Piper

SOMERLED MacDonald died in March, 1948. To me it was saddening to learn that so little was known about this artist and his work. As an artist Somerled MacDonald achieved both recognition and distinction. As a man he was gallant and kind. His friendship was unforgettable.

He came of a proud line. His father, Lachlan MacDonald, was born in Ord in 1833, and married a daughter of Captain MacLeod of Gesto, Skye, whose name was famous in the Highlands for his work in connection with Highland music — especially piobaireachd. Lachlan MacDonald became the owner of vast indigo plantations — and returned to Skye to settle at Skeabost, where Somerled was born.

Somerled received the early part of his education at Cargilfield, Midlothian, and the more advanced at the Inverness college. In spite of this town upbringing he retained a strong and very beautiful Skye accent all his days, and made use of the Skye idiom. "Have I the Gaelic? No, I have no Gaelic myself, but my father had it — and his Gaelic comes out in my English". Endowed with a quick sense of humour he enjoyed many a "crack" at himself and his locution. "You see, I was taught *English* in The Inverness College by a *German* professor. That's why I'm so good at it! 'Shall' and 'will' have always been a mystery to me and I never 'shall' or should it be 'will' master them."

If Somerled did not make much progress with his studies while at school — one thing he did do was to play his bagpipes to the boys there and so enthuse them with his music that they, too, wished to play. Under his tuition, they formed themselves into a first-class pipe band — the first pipe band ever to be recruited in any Scottish school.

It was at that great Highland social event, the Northern Meeting

Ball, that Somerled met and fell in love with Mary Lang — a daughter of the Rev. Gavin Lang of Inverness, and a relative of Cosmo Lang, Archbishop of Canterbury.

Mary Lang was something quite new in the old-fashioned town of Inverness, for she had but lately arrived from Canada, and her slight and nimble figure, with its barely eighteen-inch waist, had caused no little comment when she skated with breathtaking dexterity on the local pond. Few ladies attempted to skate in these days — and this very lovely little person with her brilliantly golden hair, and deep violet laughing eyes won many hearts.

Somerled was Catholic, and Mary, Presbyterian, so the affair was not altogether approved of — and Somerled was despatched to his father's indigo estates in India, when only seventeen years of age. Two years later, however, Mary Lang voyaged to India where they were married. A son, Lachlan, was born to them there. Seven years later they were forced to return to Britain as Somerled's health had completely broken down under the tropical heat.

It was then that he resolved to take up painting seriously, and began his studies in London. Thereafter he went to Paris to become a student at Julian's, where "it was a miracle I learned anything — packed as we were like herring in a barrel. One had to draw lots for a place — and the few in the front row were the only ones who ever saw the model, and the rest pressed so hard upon these that even these poor devils couldn't use their brushes properly — and on top of that one was nearly blinded by cigarette smoke".

Yet it was here that Somerled learned to paint — and paint so well that his work was exhibited at practically all the Continental exhibitions, and the Bavarian Government bought one of his favourite paintings, "The Piper". Returning to Scotland, he settled in Edinburgh, hoping for some sort of recognition there for his work, but none was forthcoming.

Now fate struck him a hard blow. Indigo dyes gave place to the newer and cheaper synthetic dyes, and the market for indigo collapsed, bringing the MacDonald fortunes down with it. Somerled resolved to turn his artistic ability to use. The struggle was a depressing one, and after a few disappointing years in Edinburgh he travelled north to Fortrose. Here he suffered another blow, for Lachlan, the pride and joy of his heart, suddenly died while holidaying in Skye.

For a while life became almost unbearable, but Somerled

The author, the late Miss Mairi A. MacDonald.

Inverness in days gone by.
Of the buildings seen in this picture, only the Steeple and the adjacent Court House still stand.

The corner of the High Street and Inglis Street.

The High Street in the 1920s.

The temporary bridge for traffic, used while the new bridge was being built. The older part of the Castle (1834) is on the right, the later (1846) on the left.

Somerled MacDonald, artist and piper.

Ronnie MacLennan (holding thistle) with his dance team, the Harthill Silver Thistle Dancers (1966).

Right: Founders of the Mod. The Oban men who began it all. Left to right, ex-Provost Hugh MacCowan, Councillor J.M. Campbell, Provost Dugald MacIsaac, and Mr John Campbell. It was at a meeting in John Campbell's house that the idea of a "Highland Eisteddfod" was first discussed.

Below, left: Gordon Daviot.

Below, right: Scott Skinner.

Highland Railway Engine. It appears to be Number 1 and its name, "Raigmore", commemorates one of the original committee, Mr Mackintosh of Raigmore.

02/467 4-4-0 No. 79 "Atholl" standing by the loco box at Inverness. It is decorated for moving a Royal Train, possibly to carry Queen Victoria.

The Harbour in about 1896, with a collier in the middle.

Loch Ness, a paddle steamer, tied up at Muirtown at the top of the locks.

The Sobieski Brothers
Opposite: The elder brother, John Carter Allan alias *John Hay Allan* alias *John Sobieski Stolberg Stuart.*

The Younger brother, Charles Manning Allen, alias *Charles Stuart Hay Allan* alias *Charles Edward Stuart.*

A reproduction, much reduced, of one of R.R. MacIan's illustrations for James Logan's The Clans of the Scottish Highlands *which was published in 1845. The spelling of his name was given then as R.R. McIan.*

sought consolation in his beloved bagpipes. As a younger man he had gained distinction by winning the amateur piping championship of Britain, and now he was much in demand as a judge at games all over the country.

That he knew the music as few did has never been denied, for he had inherited not only the knowledge and genius of his famous grand-uncle (Gesto), but also what amounted almost to a passion for piobaireachd and everything concerning it. It was he who first realised that the majority of pipers failed to differentiate between the playing of a lament and a salute — and that in consequence a piobaireachd was often incorrectly interpreted and in some cases quite absurdly named.

One example of this was "The Big Spree". This title worried him, for he considered the music of this piobaireachd as "the saddest music I know". Research brought to light the fact that the Catholics had adopted the word "spree" during the post-Reformation period, when the penal laws were in force, as a code word to camouflage the celebration of Mass or some such religious occasion. The beautiful, intensely sad music of the incongruously named "Big Spree" was the expression of the emotion aroused by the drama of the Last Supper.

Somerled MacDonald, too, discovered that the correct title, according to ancient "Canntaireachd" and "Joseph MacDonald's Theory" of what was erroneously named "The Lament for Viscount Dundee", and played as such, was "Thainig Gorrie" — "Welcome Gorrie" — a well-known salute. He explained also how "The Cock of the North" had completely changed its character — for as a boy he remembered his father's piper playing two tunes in the early morning when guests were taking their departure from Skeabost. One was "Cock Crowing", and the other "Lord Lovat's Lament". Both were played to express sorrow at parting.

It was found, however, that "Cock Crowing", when speeded up, became an excellent march, so excellent, in fact, that the Gordon Highlanders adopted it as their regimental march and renamed it "The Cock of the North". Yet his knowledge was not welcomed in the piping world, and rows between the judges became so frequent and so unpleasant that eventually he refused to act anywhere as a judge.

At a first meeting he appeared to be a rather autocratic, hot-tempered old gentleman, who, if annoyed, could explode into a volley of extremely expressive invective. To know the man, however, was to find someone who, at heart, was as gentle as a lamb; someone who craved for beauty and harmony in life, and whose soul oveflowed with warm kindness.

I had the good fortune often to sit with him in his studio while he painted, and as his hand carried the brush from palette to canvas his conversation accompanied its movements. Sometimes I found myself translated to India — to the life of the indigo plantation. I was introduced to such people as the letter-writer, who, with his bag of quills tied round his waist, sallied forth to pen the corres- pondence of the illiterate, "putting down any d—— thing he thought of, for his clients couldn't even read far less write"; or the wealthy potentate "who cornered rice and started up a famine where there was no need for famine at all".

Other afternoons I spent in Paris, exploring her magnificent architecture, her boulevards are her bois. It was there that I learned about a sixth sense — a sense which an artist must develop if he is to understand what the old masters knew for "composition" — a sense which anticipates emotion before it actually registers, and can weave this into the fabric of a canvas, merging colour and subject into one complete conception which expresses the artist's intention. "That's something we moderns have lost — this art of 'composition'. The old masters had it. Take Gainsborough's 'Blue Boy' for instance, who, of course, was really a girl, or Rembrandt's 'The Artist's Son, Titus', or Correggio's 'Gunymede', or Leonar- do Da Vinci's 'Mona Lisa'. They all have it. That's what makes art so interesting. It's really a great adventure. One is always finding something new. It lures one on, and never satiates — for con- tinually there is that longing, that striving for perfection, that passion to create and express the ultimate. That's what impels one to work on and on".

Often at this juncture a scraping noise outside the door heralded the arrival of Mary in her wheelchair, for over the years arthritis had crippled her once nimble limbs. As we enjoyed a cup of tea the studio would ring with her merry laughter as she described "the governor's rage when finding Alick (Matheson Lang) stampeding about in heavy, nailed boots on the top of the dining-room sideboard — the only decent piece of furniture we ever achieved — declaiming, 'Friends, Romans, countrymen' with tremendous gusto to the family, and the painful ending to this spirited performance", or some such youthful escapade, for she was eternally youthful, even at the age of eighty five.

It was at this period that fortune elected to smile again for a spell. A magnificent portrait of Lord Lovat was hung in the Royal Academy, and in consequence, orders for portraits from many Highland chiefs ensued.

During the following ten years MacDonald did much of his best work — portraits, still-life studies, flower studies and landscape. The years, however, took heavy toll of his health, and soon it became evident that something serious was amiss. Violent pain in one foot forced him to his bed. Skilled medical attention did its best, but one day it was found that the main vein in his leg had completely blocked, and an amputation became necessary.

Mary's lovely eyes were brimful of tears as she told me. "We were advised not to alarm him", she confided, "as he may not live, and he's always hated the thought of any kind of operation. The doctors told him he must go to hospital merely for treatment". Next day he was taken away, and when I called Mary was in her chair, clutching a piece of paper in her hand.

"Look at that", she said, and handed it to me. I looked, and a strange feeling stole over me, for on the sheet was drawn a figure of a man stretched on an operating table, with one leg amputated.

"We found it crumpled up, underneath his pillow, after he'd been taken to hospital", she whispered.

A few weeks later I saw him again. I shall never forget my feelings when I beheld my two dear old friends both in wheel chairs, but I was greeted with a cheery, "Come right in. They got my leg, but not my hands, and I can still paint". The easel was set up beside him, and facing me was a rough sketch of birds, "They make one think of Heaven", he mused, as he took up his charcoal. "Their symmetry and the splendour of their colouring fascinate me. There's music in it". He lived for almost a year longer, the easel beside him even when he became bedridden. The family burying ground at Portree, Skye, was his resting place.

A memorial service was held in St Andrews Cathedral, Inverness. At the conclusion of the service Pipe-Major Donald MacLeod of the Seaforth Highlanders, from a position in the corridor between the Cathedral's twin towers, played the lament, "Old Woman's Lullaby", with deeply touching effect.

Some months later his self-portrait was presented by Mary, who survived him by a few years, to the town of Inverness. Those of us who had loved him and admired his genius were met in our Town Hall, along with our Provost and Magistrates, to await the arrival

of Mary, who, brave as ever, was carried into the Council Chamber
by two attendants, and lowered into a specially prepared chair.
Their long devoted friend, the Countess of Cawdor, handed the
portrait over to the Provost, and as we gazed on the almost living
features a faint murmur reached my ears — "My old darling. I
think he knows". Somehow I felt Mary was right.

Chapter 14

The Joseph MacDonald "Theory"

THE story of Joseph MacDonald's "Compleat Theory of the Scots Highland Bagpipe" has a plot which rivals that of many a detective novel.

The Theory, compiled about 1760, was printed and published by James Johnson, Edinburgh, in 1803 — and shortly afterwards practically all trace of Joseph MacDonald and his Theory seems to have been lost. By 1927, when a copy was discovered in a saleroom in Inverness, only three other copies still extant could be found, and one of these was incomplete.

The unexpected discovery of this copy in Inverness caused quite a stir in the piping world, where it was hailed with the assurance that it would settle certain points in the execution of piobaireachd, about which the leading pipers were at variance.

In 1928, therefore, a second edition of The Theory was published by the late Mr Alex. MacDonald, who had purchased the original copy. Infinite care was exercised to provide that the new edition should be copied accurately. Mr MacDonald, unfortunately, died suddenly on the eve of this publication.

A great number of leading pipers studied the work, but all were confused and perplexed by its contents. The Theory contained written instructions with regard to the playing of the bagpipes, and examples of the various types of bagpipe music, complete with the intricate variations of the piobaireachd.

These written directives were illustrated by staff-notation examples of the music referred to, but the written directive and the staff-notation failed to agree. Further, there was frequent use of a Gaelic term "Iuludh", which I could not trace in any dictionary.

The concensus of opinion was that Joseph must have been an extremely careless notation scribe — so careless, in fact, that the work was worthless and should therefore be returned to the limbo where it had already been for over a century.

The more I studied the meticulous accuracy of the written word, however, the more I became convinced that Joseph was anything but a careless student of his subject, and that there must be some very adequate explanation of the highly unintelligent work that was in his Theory. My first step in the solution of the mystery was to find out everything possible about this man — Joseph MacDonald.

Joseph MacDonald, I learned, was one of the sons of the Rev. Murdoch MacDonald, minister of Durness, Sutherland. The Rev. Murdoch, a man of no mean ability himself, as is evident from his translation of a large portion of Pope's works into Gaelic, had been gifted with a marvellous singing voice, a voice of such unusual power and timbre, that it could be heard, leading his congregation in its praise, far and wide over the rugged Durness hills.

His own deep love of music engendered in him a desire to develop musical taste in the members of his family. The bagpipes and the violin were the instruments he favoured, but more especially the bagpipes, which, as a contemporary of the later MacCrimmons, he considered to be the medium of expression of all that was finest in our Highland culture.

There were two particularly promising musical members of his family — the older, Patrick, who published his "Collection of Highland Vocal Airs" in 1784, and the younger, Joseph, eventually acknowledged as a musical genius. To advance the musical knowledge of these two, the Rev. Murdoch employed Kenneth Sutherland, Cnocbrec, a noted exponent of our native music.

When Joseph was about sixteen he was sent to Haddington for further education, and here he devoted most of his leisure to music and painting. From Haddington he went to Edinburgh, where, under the tutelage of the renowned Signor Pasquali, celebrated for his compositions inspired by Shakespeare's "The Tempest" and "Romeo and Juliet", and other famous masters, he enjoyed an exceptional and extensive musical education.

Although Joseph loved Italian music, he loved his native music above all other, and upon his return to Strathnaver, some years later, gave all his attention to its study. He collected and noted down all the airs he could glean — especially those suitable for the bagpipe. During this period, owing to the proscription of the bagpipes after the Battle of Culloden, it was unlawful for a

Highlander to play the bagpipes. At this time, however, Joseph, like his brother, by now the Rev. Patrick MacDonald of Kilmore, Argyllshire, was considered to be a Lowlander, and as a son of the manse could enjoy a freedom denied to most of his contemporaries. Thus he was allowed to pursue his favourite study unmolested.

In 1760 he went to the East Indies to work with The East India Company, but before leaving home completed a copy of his choice native airs, which Patrick incorporated into his "Collection of Highland Vocal Airs".

The following extract from one of Joseph's own letters to his father after his arrival in the East gives us an illuminating glimpse of his character and ambitions.

"There is nothing brings to my mind a more natural and soothing joy than the playing and fingering our sweet Highland luinings (ditties), jorrams (rowing songs) etc., when by myself, for alas! I have none capable of sharing the pleasure with me. They paint afresh the many innocent and sweet scenes of my rural and puerile life, far beyond description. What would I give now, far from the theatre of those delightful scenes, for one night of my own beloved society to sing those favourite, simple, primitive airs along with me? It would bring me back to the golden age anew. O! that I had been more at pains to gather those admirable remains of our ancient Highland music before I left my native country. It would have augmented my collection of Highland music and poetry, which I have formed a system of in my voyage to India, and purpose to send home soon, dedicated to Sir James MacDonald, or some such chief of high rank and figure in the Highlands, in order that those sweet, noble and expressive sentiments of nature may not be allowed to sink and die away, and to show that our poor, remote corner, even without the advantage of learning and cultivation, abounded in works of taste and genius".

Fate intervened at this date, however, and with cruel hand snatched away this genius from our midst, for Joseph MacDonald died in the East Indies of a malignant fever when only twenty-three years of age. His effects, including the manuscript of The Theory were collected and brought home to his brother Patrick by a fellow bagpipe enthusiast, Sir John Murray MacGregor.

A letter, written by Robert Burns to Mrs Dunlop of Dunlop, revealed that the poet had composed his "Song of Death", to one of Joseph's Highland airs.

Another letter, written by Mr J. Ramsay to the Rev. W. Young, testified that Robert Burns had been very much delighted with the Highland airs collected by Joseph, and also confirmed that Joseph and his works were held in high esteem by his contemporaries.

In consideration of these facts, how could I agree that a man of such ability and repute could have allowed this travesty to flow from his pen?

My next move, in the hope of solving the mystery, was to try to discover the original manuscript of the Theory. I learned of the existence of such a manuscript from a distinguished member of the Piobaireachd Society, who had often handled it, in the Signet Library, Edinburgh, in his student days. Over the years this manuscript had mysteriously disappeared. I felt I must try some fresh approach.

Quite unexpectedly the first clue to the mystery presented itself when I was reading a chapter on Scottish music in Logan's "The Scottish Gael" (1878). I read:—

"The appoggiaturas in modern music are usually the next in degree to the chief note, and any great departure from this rule is accounted a barbarism. In Scots music they are some degree distant, and appear very graceful. This is most remarkable in pipe tunes, to which instrument they are indispensable".

I reflected that in his preface to "The Collection of Highland Vocal Airs", Patrick had shown himself rather averse to the use of the appoggiatura — that small note, but for its tiny tail, almost indistinguishable from a grace note, which could be of any length — minim, crotchet or quaver — the rule being that it should take its own value from the note that it preceded, generally one half.

Was it possible that Joseph's original notation had been tampered with before publication, and that the meddler had mixed up those two musical ornaments, substituting appoggiaturas — notes of definite length — for grace notes, which know no time value, and are produced by a mere flick of the finger? If so, who was responsible for this tampering?

I applied the supposition that Joseph's grace notes had been treated as appoggiaturas, and calculated how the staff-notation extracts should have been noted in such a circumstance. To my joy I found that I had discovered that this was the fundamental error that underlay all the "careless" work of the Theory. Had the "ornaments" been read as grace-notes, and the staff noted accordingly, written directives and staff-notation would have agreed.

The fly-leaf of the Theory, dedicating the work to Sir John Murray MacGregor of MacGregor, bore the printed signature of Patrick MacDonald. How, I argued, could Patrick MacDonald, an eminent and educated musician, have been guilty of a mistake such as this? His own work, from which it was clear that he knew all there was to know about the use of appoggiaturas and grace-notes, rendered the charge ridiculous.

I re-applied myself to the Introduction in the Theory, addressed "To The Public". Here, after a short description of the work of Joseph MacDonald, was a discourse upon bagpipe and harp music. Then followed a strange digression:—

"In the days of Fingal the dirge appears to have been accompanied by the Harp, which is peculiarly suited to the tender and pathetic emotions. It is supposed to be of greater antiquity than the bagpipe, because this last is neither mentioned nor alluded to in any of the poems of Ossian, which of all the Highland compositions that have reached us, are certainly the most ancient; and the sublime, and the unequalled original, with its translation, which on the whole is excellent will continue to be admired by men of refined genius and taste, for ages after the silly cavils of illiberal sceptics, as grossly ignorant of that living language of their country, as superlatively confident in groundless assertions, shall, at best, be consigned to oblivion".

Why, I ruminated, should the writer of this Introduction digress from his subject, and make opportunity for such an oration in praise of Ossian's work and its translation?

I had just communicated my discovery to those interested when still more exciting news came to hand. It was now 1947, and Edinburgh was preparing for the first Festival. The different libraries had been invited to contribute any very interesting old manuscript in their possession, and what had turned up amongst those lent by the University Library, was the manuscript of Joseph MacDonald's Theory!

No time was lost in getting to Edinburgh to examine "the find". The member of The Piobaireachd Society already referred to as having often seen the manuscript in his student days was the first to inspect it, and almost stunned those present by immediately declaring that this was not the manuscript he had handled before.

The only conclusion possible was that there must have been *two* manuscripts.

There, in front of us, lay a medium-sized notebook, bound in glazed black covers, the pages of which, cut from paper of Dutch manufacture extensively used in the 18th century, were covered with closely written copper plate, and neatly constructed notation tables. An introductory page, in the same hand-writing had been gummed into the manuscript, set out word for word as was the one in the printed edition. On the last page was a coloured sketch of a Highland piper playing a three-droned bagpipe, each finger correctly placed on the chanter. This was obviously the work of a piper and an artist — the work of Joseph himself. We had before us Joseph's original manuscript of his Theory.

An examination of its pages quickly cleared up the mystery of the unknown term "Iuludh". Joseph's faultless copperplate revealed that the word should have been "Tuludh", a term well-known amongst pipers. Further discrepancies manifested themselves as we turned the pages — a notable one being that the description of the three-droned bagpipe which we found in the printed copy was not included in the manuscript.

The work was undoubtedly the work of a genius — careful, neat and inspired. Faultlessly accurate notation tables agreed in every case with the written directive, and so ably was the work executed that the music simply leapt at one to explain and express all the intricacies of this wonderful instrument. The use of appoggiaturas had in every case been avoided. Now it was clear that the Theory we had known had been printed from that second manuscript which had gone astray, and that the manuscript had without doubt been prepared by someone other than Joseph or Patrick, for Patrick must have known his brother's handrwriting far too well to mistake a "T" for an "I".

Idly turning the pages back again, we found ourselves re-reading this Introduction, so we turned yet another page prior to where the Introduction had been inserted, and there we saw what made us all gasp — "Eldin, 1833".

Quickly we sought out the librarian. Immediately he satisfied our questioning. The MS. was acquired by the Library from the estate of a collector, Mr D. Laing, who had bought it in 1833 at the sale of Lord Eldin's Collection.

John Clerk, Lord Eldin, like his father and grandfather, was an Antiquary, and a firm friend of Dr Blair — champion of Ossian's poems and their translation by MacPherson. We now know that Ossian's Poems were made up from multiple fragments of ancient Gaelic poetry, strung together into long complete poems, whose authenticity was everywhere doubted by Gaelic scholars. Now we were again confronted by the dubious work of these antiquaries. The unnecessary laudation of Ossian's Poems and their translation amounting almost to advertisement, contained in the preface "To the Public" confirmed this. At last the mystery was solved.

Patrick, at the time of the publication of his brother's Theory (1803) was seventy-four years of age — an old man, and none too rich. His own "Vocal Airs" had been financed by subscribers, a list of whom is found at the beginning of the volume. It would seem that anxious to have the Theory published, he handed it over with a letter of dedication to the antiquaries. Not knowing much about Bagpipe music they had employed some "hack" whose identity will perchance never be discovered to "dress up" the manuscript for publication. This person, mistakenly under the impression that Joseph's notation must be old-fashioned, tried to alter it into the more fashionable notation of his own day with the disastrous results that confront us in the printed Theory.

The first manuscript found which had eventually gone astray was that of this "hack". We are now, however, in possession of Joseph's own manuscript, accurate and illuminating in every detail — a monument to the genius of one whose work has survived death and time.

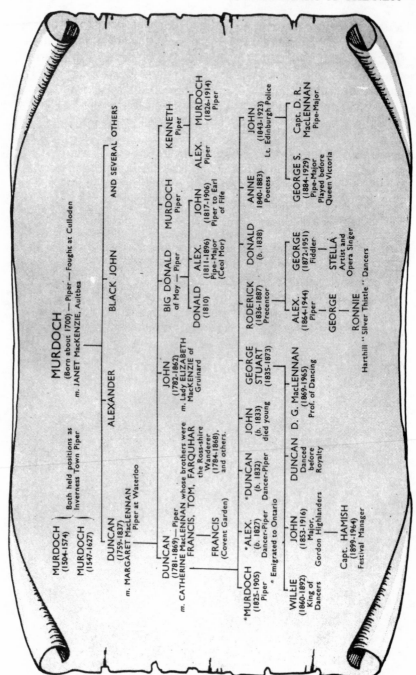

Chapter 15

A Remarkable Family Tree

AS I watched The Silver Thistle Dancers I was somehow whisked back into the long ago. Stage, audience, and orchestra faded from the picture, leaving only dancers who, in their neat steps, elegant postures, and lively swings recaptured that vital spirit which is so essential an ingredient of real old Highland dancing. Who had trained them?

I sat up with a start as a kilted man addressed me. "I was wondering how they came to be so good. Who trained them?" I asked.

"I did. I'm Ronnie MacLennan".

"Any relation of the dancing and piping MacLennans of old?"

"I'm one of them. Are you interested in family trees?"

"Very. Have you one?"

"Yes, and I'll show it to you some day".

That was my introduction to Ronnie MacLennan. Months later Ronnie visited me in Inverness, bringing his tree and family album along with him. As we pored over these, two and a half centuries seemed to slip away.

I found it was possible to trace this MacLennan family back to the beginning of the eighteenth century, to one, Murdoch, a piper, born about 1700, who later fought at Culloden. There was, to my amazement, a link between this man and two other MacLennan pipers — one Murdoch (1504-1574) and a second Murdoch (1547-1627), who had held positions as town pipers in Inverness — the latter being killed in a raid by retainers of the Earl of Moray. The two would, in all probability, have played the earlier two-droned bagpipe, and passed their musical knowledge on to their kinsmen, who developed the art.

It was believed in the district that the family originally came from Strathconon. Descendants still have a snuff-box and a well used bone *cuachan**, inscribed "Alex MacLennan, Strathconon, 1784".

* Small drinking cup.

Murdoch lived at Mellon Charles — "Charles's little hill" —
Ross-shire, and married Janet MacKenzie, Tighnafiline — House
of the Shorefield — Aultbea. These two had for family — Duncan,
who married Margaret MacLennan; Alexander, Black John and
several others. Of these, Duncan was the most adventuresome.
Taught to play the pipes by Angus MacKay, he joined the
renowned "Freiceadan Dubh" — Black Watch. In 1779 he piped
at the head of fifty recruits who were marching from Stirling to
Leith for embarkation — but who, when told that they were to be
drafted to a non-Highland regiment, mutinied. In the fracas
which followed, he was wounded in the leg. Later, however, he
distinguished himself as one of the pipers whose skirl persisted at
Waterloo, wherever fire was hottest.

Duncan and Margaret had a largish family — Duncan, who
married Catherine MacLennan, a midwife, two of whose
brothers, Francis and Tom, were singers. Francis emigrated in
the 1860 evictions, and his son, Francis, born in Michigan, sang in
the Covent Garden Opera Company, London, between 1889 and
1893. Thomas MacLennan of Neil and MacLennan's well-known
music shop, which flourished in Inverness in the '20s, was connected with this branch of the family. Another brother of Catherine's was Farquhar, the Ross-shire Wanderer.

Their second son, John, married Lady Elizabeth MacKenzie of
Gruinard. He was her senior by twenty-five years, and after his
death at Mellon Charles in 1862, she emigrated to Australia, about
1870, to join her family who had gone out earlier. Their third son,
Big Donald of Moy, also a piper, had three sons, Donald, Alex.
and John. Of these, Alex. was pipe-major of the Inverness Militia,
and is mentioned by General Thomason in the preface to his *Ceol
Mor*, and John became piper to the Earl of Fife.

Murdoch, Duncan's fourth son, was a piper, as was Kenneth,
the youngest, who was the father of Murdoch, the famous Munlochy piper, born in 1826, winner at the Northern Meeting in
Inverness in 1862. The bagpipes used on this occasion, given to
him by John Ban MacKenzie, are held by a family descendant to
this day, and bear a plate with the inscription:

By the Northern Meeting
to Murdoch MacLennan,
Piper to the Munlochy Rifle Corps
for best performance of the
Great Highland Bagpipe. Sept. 1862

Exceptionally tall, and, as he became old — for he lived to be 88 years of age — picturesque in appearance, with his long, flowing white beard, Murdoch was a well-known figure in Artafallie, near Munlochy, where he lived for a while and later at Gairnside, near Lentran, and Bogallan, where he died. His lame brother, Alex. of Tore, was also a well-known piper.

Duncan, a tailor-crofter, born at Aultbea, "the gentle slope", did not emigrate, though a Waterloo medal, 1815, found amongst his possessions would suggest that he, too, had fought in this memorable battle. He and Catherine, in their turn, reared a large family, eight sons, all pipers and dancers, and one daughter Anne, a poetess, whose poems "Sacred and Secular", published in Edinburgh in 1884, I have before me now.

A preface by the late Rev. J. Kennedy, D.D., Dingwall, tells that Anne was born in Resolis in April 1840 and moved to Killearnan four years later, where she was educated. When old enough she went to Perth, and was for some time a domestic servant in a manse there. She then accepted the appointment of Bible Woman in Lochgilphead, and there, in household visitation of the poor, she spent the later years of her life and wrote her poems.

These poetical pieces are deeply evangelical and surprisingly enlightened, giving a sharp picture of a wonderfully cultured woman who truly believed in her God. She died in September 1883.

Logan, in his *Scottish Gael*, mentions Duncan's two eldest boys, Murdoch and Alex. in connection with the "Dirk Dance", which, he tells us, was last performed in London in 1850 by these two MacLennan brothers, who by then were the only individuals who could dance it. This "Dirk Dance" which must not be confused with today's "Sword Dance", was the original "Dannsadh na Biodaig", a kind of pyrrhic dance which depicted thrust and attack on the part of the dancer, who eventually worked himself up into a battle frenzy.

Duncan's youngest son, John, born at Mulbuie, Kilcoy, in 1843, became a lieutenant in the Edinburgh Police, and during his lifetime was one of the foremost authorities on pipe music and an expert teacher of the bagpipe. As lieutenant in the chargeroom, he gradually won for himself a reputation for his knowledge of criminal law, after gaining a high place in this subject in the university.

When in 1906 he retired from police service he devoted all his energies to his piping, publishing in 1907 *The Piobaireachd As MacCrimmon Played It*. In 1914, although 71 years of age, he volunteered to help his country, and was appointed to a recruiting post at Falkirk, which he held until 1916. In recognition of his services he received the army rank of Hon. Lieutenant. Peace found him once again engrossed in his hobby, and a further publication, *Collection of Pibrochs, Marches, and Two Reels*, soon appeared. He died in Edinburgh in 1923.

Lieut. MacLennan had several children, the most outstanding of whom was George S. MacLennan of the Gordon Highlanders. George inherited a wealth of traditional piping knowledge, and early showed his genius by winning both the Amateur Championship of Scotland and the Open Championship of London twice before he was 11 years of age. These were the outstanding events in a host of lesser gains, and there was that thrilling moment when Queen Victoria, a great lover of bagpipe music herself, expressed an ardent wish to hear the "marvellous boy who could express on his tuneful pipes songs that men who had laboured to do could not better".

The mighty (Donald Mor) MacCrimmon had been an old man when he stood before King Charles II in 1651 as the King of Pipers. Two centuries later his place was taken by a boy of ten who played by request before his Queen.

In 1899 George, aged 15, joined the Gordon Highlanders, and three years later was promoted to the rank of pipe-major. He continued to compete at all piping competitions — in Inverness, Oban, Crieff, Fort William, Bridge of Allan, Braemar and Portree — and when he died in 1929 at the early age of 45 his quiver of honours was full and overflowing — 2800 cups, medals, and prizes having been won during these years. The Kemble Star, gifted by Col. Kemble of Knock, was his most prized trophy, valued not so much for the handsome medal as for his great affection for the donor.

But not only was George an outstanding piper, he was a composer also, two of his favourite compositions, *Bogallan* and *Gairnside*, being dedicated to his ancestor Murdoch, the Munlochy piper, winner at the Northern Meeting of 1862. Another composition in memory of a relative was *Major John MacLennan*. His jacket and medals are housed in the Military Museum, Edinburgh Castle.

George's brother, Pipe-Major D.R. MacLennan of the Seaforth

Highlanders, also occupies a leading position in the piping world. In 1920 he won an open competition at the Northern Meeting at Inverness, but by the end of the second war felt that his competition days were over. His friends, however, persuaded him to return to the piping arena, and at Lochearnhead Games in 1955 he won the open piobaireachd competition and the bronze star of the Royal Scottish Piper's Society. Thereafter he went from strength to strength, winning many prizes, and climaxing a brilliant career by winning the gold medal for piobaireachd at Oban and the similar trophy at the Northern Meeting, Inverness, within a week of each other, in 1956.

Lieut. John MacLennan also taught his nephew William, whom he took into his own family on the death of the boy's father. Another uncle, Murdo MacLennan, taught the young nephew dancing. After leaving school Willie became a newspaper reporter before turning to architecture, of which he became a fully qualified practitioner. During these pursuits he continued with his piping and dancing, and also studied ballet in Paris.

On his return to Scotland he made radical changes in the style of Highland dancing, which were acclaimed great improvements and quickly adopted by the leading dancers of that day. Forming his own concert party, which included Scott Skinner, the well-known violinist, he made three tours of the United States and Canada, teaching dancing in Montreal during several winters, where he also conducted art classes in painting and drawing. An impressive setting of his for reels was the deck of a ship, the dancers dipping torches in a paraffin drum and carrying these as they danced, the bright flames silhouetted against sky and water.

He won all the piping and dancing honours of his day, including the Highland Society of London Medal at the Argyllshire Gathering in 1875, and also at Inverness in 1879. An amusing story is told of him, when competing at the Balmoral Gathering in 1887. He had won all the firsts in open dancing, and knowing himself to be the best piper present, was surprised to find himself placed second. He immediately asked the judges what mistake he had made.

"Oh, nae mistake. You played capital".

"Surely, then, I was entitled to first prize".

"Maybe ye wis — but ye see, ye had a' the firsts for dancing".

"But was I not the best dancer?"

"Nae doot about that".

"And was I not the best piper, too?"

"We're no' saying but ye wis".

"But I thought the best piper ought to get first prize".

"Oh, nae doot, but we thought ye had gotten plenty already".

"I wonder what they would have done if the competitor was a hammer-thrower or a jumper", Willie mused. "They could not say 30 ft. was less than 25 ft. — or perhaps they could".

When Willie died in Montreal General Hospital, in October, 1892, at the early age of thirty-two, the newspaper carried the caption, "King of Dancers Dead".

Willie's brother, Donald G. MacLennan, Professor of Dancing, born at Minard Castle in 1869, where his father was estate manager, became a member of the Examining Committee of the Association of Operatic Dancing of Great Britain, and one of the examiners at the Royal Academy, London. His style expertly polished by Dame Adeline Genee and her uncle, the famous Danish *maitre de ballet*, Alexander Genee, he edited *Highland and Traditional Scottish Dances* in 1950. He died 1965 in his 96th year.

Another brother, Duncan, also born at Minard Castle, danced before Royalty. Yet another brother, John, Major in the Gordon Highlanders, who was killed in 1916, was the father of Captain Hamish MacLennan who was first manager of Edinburgh Festival.

Every self-respecting family tree must have a black sheep hidden somewhere amongst its branches — and we find a very interesting member of this species in the MacLennan one. I refer to "Fearchair-a-Ghunna", "Farquhar of the Gun" — the Ross-shire Wanderer.

Farquhar, born in 1784 in Strathconon, of a family of smugglers, was the uncle of Lieutenant John MacLennan. His father was a well-to-do crofter, but Farquhar early in life proved himself to be, to say the least of it, rather difficult. In appearance he was smallish, but sturdily built with square shoulders and a remarkably erect gait. His head was covered with a profusion of long bristly hair — seldom if ever combed — his eyes, small, restless, and piercing, while a fixed determination was stamped on his careworn countenance.

As a youth he had been engaged as a herd with a man named Gray, at Croftruny, in the parish of Redcastle. One warm summer day found him fast asleep — his cattle having strayed into a nearby cornfield. His master — furious with his herd, hit him a blow on the side of his head with a spade, which broke his collar-bone and severely gashed his face.

At this time the Excise officers were very specifically engaged in routing out the Strathconon smugglers, and had procured a cottage in the district from which to operate. One morning the cottage was found burnt to the ground, and everyone knew that Farquhar had had some hand in this. He was taken to Dingwall for examination, where one of the Excisemen, hoping to frighten him into a confession, threatened to cut his head off with his cutlass if he wouldn't give the desired information. Farquhar's answer was "You may get all the information from my head that you can, but you will get none from me".

After losing a favourite brother in an accident with the gaugers, and seeing his old father apprehended for smuggling, one fine day in 1809 Farquar left his home, and began his nomadic existence. He set himself up as a gentleman-at-large, to entertain whom should be considered an honour.

His favourite haunt was the Black Isle, where, festooned by heavy chains, bits of rags, feathers, and wisps of paper, he soon became a well-kent figure. A large sack of his own peculiar treasures was carried on his back, while a brace of castaway pistols hung from his iron belt, which also anchored a Mexican powder-horn, several iron hoops, pieces of chain, a sword, and a bunch of keys.

His most treasured possession, however, was his gun, which was of most wonderful and unusual construction. It was made up of about half a dozen old gun barrels, tied together with a chain, and embedded in a stock which he himself had carved out of the thick end of a tree. This monster weapon was too heavy to use at the shoulder, so he made a rest for it, and carried also a pan with a burning peat within to ignite the powder. Before action he first got the gun adjusted on the rest to the requisite level, then he laid a train of powder to each of the barrels, and lastly applied the peat. The six barrels went off simultaneously with a terrific report — but nothing aimed at was ever hit!

Farquhar was an old man when first he saw the railway — and did not realise that he needed a ticket for travel. Having been unceremoniously dragged from a carriage by a ticket-collector, he remarked amusedly — "This road reminds me of the Lord's Table — no one being permitted to take it, unless he is provided with a token or ticket".

Wandering about the countryside he lived on dead crows, frogs, and any dead game he happened to come across. To earn a penny to buy his gunpowder, he would repeat his own original prayer, which began—

"O blessed Trinity, Thou art in America and Australia, and Thou are here just now. Thou art like the fish on the hook — the high tide will not let Thee off. O Thou art the Blessed Trinity. Thou art here just now, and Thou art in the Highlands, and in Inverness, and on the high steeples. Thou art here just now, and east at Tain. Thou art giving slated houses to the big folk, but Thou hast only given a black sooty bothy to me, which won't keep out a raindrop — every drop falling into Farquhar's gruel."

Farquhar died in Inverness Infirmary in 1868, and was buried in Tomnahurich Cemetery.

To come back now to Ronnie, with whom I began this article. He is a great-grandson of Roderick, a grandson of the first Duncan. Roderick was tall, red-haired, and nicknamed "The Minister" on account of his wisdom. Both he and his father were precentors as well as pipers and dancers. Roderick's eldest son, Alex., Ronnie's grandfather, was a judge of piping and dancing. The other members of his family were all musical, two daughters becoming music teachers.

How this tree had grown and spread over the centuries! Peeping out here and there were names such as Pipe-Major Lewis MacLennan, founder of the Police Band in Melbourne, Australia, who died there aged 77, and Duncan MacLennan, a famous Highland dancer who danced before Royalty and died in Gisborne, Wellington, New Zealand at the age of 72. And on a branch of Roderick's is Stella, opera singer and artist, whose gigantic murals in Goldberg's, Glasgow, delight all customers today.

"There's certainly no doubt it's in your blood", I said as I handed the tree back to Ronnie. "Where do you go from here?"

"To my home in Shieldaig to learn about some of our long-lost dances. Do you know anything about these?"

"Oh, yes. There's the *Cailleach an Dùrdain*. This was danced by a man and woman, and during the performance the woman falls and pretends she has been killed by the man, but he brings her to life again by breathing upon her and touching her. Then there was *An Dubh Luidneach*, a comic solo dance; the *Dannsadh na Gòraig* (Foolish Woman's Dance); the *Dannsadh nam Boc* (Dance of the Bucks); in which three men reel about fantastically imitating bucks; *Figh an Gùn* (Weave the Gown); *Croit an Droigheann* (The Thorny Croft); *Dannsadh na Tunnaig* (The Duck's Dance); *Cath nan Coileach* (Cock-fighting); *Ruidhleadh nan Coileach-dubha* (The Black Cock Dance); and one that would have delighted Black Sheep Farquhar, *Faigh an Gunna* (Get the Gun)."

Ronnie laughed. "If only I could resuscitate some of these".

"Why not, Ronnie Mor? The tree could do with another King of Dancers in this generation. Here's wishing you luck".

Chapter 16

The Mod

ON September 13, 1892, the first Mod was held in Oban. The event was the culmination of over a hundred years of what must often have seemed hopeless endeavour, in London, Glasgow and Inverness, to save the Gaelic language, its literature and music from extinction.

The first positive achievement had come in 1871, when the Gaelic Society of Inverness was instituted and, linking up with the Gaelic Societies of London and Glasgow, helped wage the successful campaign, led by Professor John Stuart Blackie, for the founding of a Celtic chair in Edinburgh University. In 1878 a petition signed by various societies and a motion led in the House of Commons by Charles Fraser-MacKintosh, M.P., Inverness, resulted in permission being granted for Gaelic to be taught in schools.

The origin of An Comunn Gaidhealach* may be traced to discussions which took place early in 1890 in Oban, between Provost Dugald MacIsaac, John Campbell, and Inverness-born John MacMaster Campbell, Sheriff-Substitute of Argyllshire. These men felt that something less academic and more popular than was being done was needed to revive the Gaelic language.

At this point Fate intervened, and out of the blue came their inspiration. In 1890, Professor Masson, of the chair of English Literature at Edinburgh, visited the Welsh Eisteddfod, and was so impressed that he wrote a spirited letter to an Edinburgh newspaper, urging the formation of a similar festival in the Scottish Highlands.

Our Oban friends reinforced by ex-Provost Hugh McCowan and H. G. Clements, an Englishman who was organist in the

*The Highland Society, formed 1891. It organises the Mod.

Pro-Cathedral, Oban, took up the challenge. In 1890 an informal meeting, held in John Campbell's house, pressed for a national festival on lines similar to those of the Welsh Eisteddfod. A hostile press immediately poured scorn on the whole idea, scathingly noting that there was not even a word in the Gaelic language to describe the proposed gathering, referred to by its promoters by the hybrid non-Gaelic name of "The Highland Eisteddfod."

This set the heather on fire. Professor Blackie appealed to all Highlanders to "put their hands and hearts to the work." Names were suggested in plenty — The Highland Bardic Association; The Highland Association; Comhfharpais nam Bard — Bard's Competition; and Mod-Ciuil (Friendly Gathering). Then the vice-president, Magnus MacLean, had a brainwave — why not simply "Mod"?

From that moment this small word took on the new and unique meaning not only of an assembly, but of a great meeting of friends, where traditions, memories, old songs, poetry, tunes, everything associated with that happy old Highland life so dear to the native could have expression.

Inverness Gaelic Society, which had always shown itself suspicious of the new movement, expressed disapproval of the name Mod, objecting that it resembled too nearly the Saxon word "moot," and suggesting the use of the word "Coinne," — a party. Mod, however, won the day, and with less than £50 in hand, the promoters advertised their venture.

The sun shone brightly as the rather apathetic Oban townsfolk strolled to the Argyllshire Gathering Hall to listen to the competitors at this first Mod. The promoters, led by their doughty president, Lord Archibald Campbell, mounted the platform with confidence, for prior to this Lord Archibald had won his spurs in defending the tartan. When the Cameron Highlanders returned from foreign service in 1877, the War Office threatened their identity. In Stafford House in 1881, Lord Archibald and other Scottish nobles present kissed the dirk as a pledge of their determination to resist the proposed changes, with the result that authority retracted, and the distinctive clan tartans were saved for the various Highland regiments.

The opening speeches over, the competitors, woefully few in number, began their recitals. The audience was obviously bored. The promoters' spirits sank. Was the whole thing to be a fiasco? Then Mr Neil Ross, Glendale, in full Highland dress, entered the

arena, and in ringing tones recited *Am Faigh a' Ghàidhlig Bàs*. The
burden of this poem is that the Gaelic shall not die — and so
dramatic was Mr Ross's recitation that all present, Gaelic-
speaking and non-Gaelic-speaking alike — rose up, applauding
enthusiastically — the cheers echoing and re-echoing through the
hall.

That evening the Gaelic concert was attended by members of
the Royal Family in the persons of Princess Louise and the
Marquis of Lorne. Miss Jessie N. MacLachlan, who, the previous
week had sung Gaelic songs by request to Queen Victoria at
Balmoral Castle, was one of the artistes. After the concert, all who
had taken part were piped from the hall by the Inveraray Pipe
Band to the Alexandra Hotel, where they were the guests at dinner
of Lord Archibald Campbell. That night it was agreed to hold a
second Mod the following year, and to extend the competitions to
junior choirs and singers — something which was made possible
by a new musical development.

In 1857 John Curwen, a young Nonconformist minister, de-
monstrated his tonic sol-fa system to a large audience in London.
By this system people who had never had the privilege of musical
education could be taught to sing. Using this system, young folk
were trained to sing Gaelic songs. We in Inverness were particularly fortunate in having the assistance of Mr Roddie, choirmaster of
the Free High Church and pioneer of the sol-fa system in the
North. So successful was his work that he was known as "the man
who taught the Highlanders to sing."

The first three Mods were held in Oban — and then it was felt
that the Mod should change its venue each year. In 1895 it was
held in Glasgow, and in 1896 in Perth — by which time it was
possible to donate £50 from funds for the travelling expenses of the
choirs and to include duets and quartettes in the syllabus.

On September 15, 1897 — the day before the first day of the
Northern Meeting Games — the Mod came to Inverness. Dr
Charles Fraser-MacKintosh presided and delegates from the Irish
Feis-Ceoil and the Welsh Eisteddfod were present and gave
addresses. The competitions were held in the Town Hall, and
during the day Dr Fraser-MacKintosh entertained 300 guests at
his beautiful seat, Lochardil. The evening concert was presided
over by Lord Lovat — a brilliant gathering with the most varied
and attractive programme ever presented at a Highland concert.

For the first twelve years the leaders of An Comunn concentrated on an annual Mod and little else. Though the beautiful Gaelic music and poetry had won the hearts of many, the growth of the movement had been slow. In 1904, after thirteen years of work and propaganda, An Comunn had only twenty-seven life members, one hundred and sixty-four ordinary members, and twelve affiliated societies. It was felt that something further must be done.

Two brilliant women — Miss Ella C. Carmichael (later wife of Dr Watson, the renowned Celtic scholar) and Mrs Margaret Burnley Campbell, of Ormidale, one of the greatest leaders An Comunn ever had, rose to the occasion. Between 1902 and 1914 the membership of the Association swelled to over two thousand, and there were almost a hundred branches throughout the land.

The twelfth annual Mod was held in the Music Hall, Inverness, in September 1903, when the Mod Concert attracted such a large audience that hundreds had to be turned away. It was then decided to make it a two-day affair the following year, and by 1906 it had become a three-day event.

In 1907 a great three-day feill (bazaar) was held in Glasgow, from which An Comunn benefited by £8000. The highlight of the feill was "An Clachan," a typical Highland village in miniature, with a background of the hills of Kintail, Loch Duich, and Eilean Donan Castle.

A full-time secretary and organiser for An Comunn was appointed in 1908, and attention was directed to the development of Highland home industries, arts and crafts. An unremitting campaign was waged to have Gaelic taught in Highland schools, and an annual summer school was begun. In addition to the official magazine "An Deo Gréine" (The Sunbeam) — the title having been taken from the name of the banner of the hero Fionn — several other publications were issued, and all the time, year after year, the Mod increased in size and popularity.

Dr Watson pointed out in 1909 that there was still a large area untapped by An Comunn — Sutherland, Lewis (with the exception of Stornoway) Skye, and most of Inverness-shire. The movement had been confined too much to Argyll. These other regions must be brought in, too. This was done, and in 1912, the year of its majority, the Mod again came to Inverness.

This Mod was indeed a memorable one — the first to receive Royal recognition. At the Thursday evening's concert Lord Lovat read a message of congratulations from the King on the celebration of the twenty-first anniversary of An Comunn's foundation.

Vigorous propaganda had been carried on in the glens and straths near Inverness by a band of indefatigable workers, of whom Dr William MacKay, the Mod president; Miss Kate Fraser, headmistress of Farraline Park School; Mr Roderick MacLeod, the premier Gaelic singer of the day, and Mr Alexander MacDonald (my own father) were the most prominent. A feature of this Mod was the very high standard of the singing of all competitors in choirs, solos, duets, and quartettes.

All over, the Mod of 1912 gave the impression that there was now sincere enthusiasm for Gaelic music and literature, controlled by a highly efficient organisation. In his speech the president told how, at the first Mod in 1892, there had been only ten competitions and £34 15s for prize money. That day there were seventy-two competitions and over £200 for prize money, as well as books, medals, pendants, the "Oban Times" Challenge Trophy, and the Lovat and Tullibardine Shield.

After the concert a ball, numbering over five hundred, was held in the Northern Meeting Rooms, at which the pipes of the Third Battalion Queen's Own Cameron Highlanders played for some of the dances. It is interesting to note that the winners of the male voice choir competition were the men of the depot Queen's Own Cameron Highlanders — the first military Mod choir, which was inaugurated by one of their officers — Major, later Colonel, Gilbert Gunn.

The Great War broke upon the country in 1914, and the Gaelic cause suffered a heavy blow. Afterwards An Comunn slowly picked up the broken strands of its many associations. The Mod returned to Inverness in September 1923, and was convened by my father. Lasting for four days, there were numerous competitions, but the perfection of the 1912 performance was not realised. A second feill in 1927 augmented the funds by £10,000.

Scarcely twelve years later a second World War dealt another heavy blow — but again An Comunn, fired perchance by the story of Van der Broeck, met the challenge with renewed vigour. The Belgian Van der Broeck had been a refugee in the Hebrides during the first war, and had learned Gaelic before returning to his own country. In the second war he was a Resistance hero and a number one suspect on the Gestapo lists. The enemy could never catch him, however, for when the nine o'clock evening news in English came over the air he was always seen out walking about the streets.

The Germans did not realise that at a quarter to eleven he listened in to the news in Gaelic — the gist of which he regularly passed on to his fellow Resistance workers.

Some first-class vocalists graced Mod platforms in the following years, such as the late James MacPhee, and Evelyn Campbell, Alasdair Gillies, Calum Kennedy and his wife, Anne, and Kenneth Macrae. A third feill in 1950 raised about £8000 for the War Memorial and Thanksgiving Fund.

In 1955 the Queen Mother and Princess Margaret attended the Mod held in Aberdeen, the Queen Mother presenting the prizes. Later she sent a message to Neil Shaw, the president, expressing their enjoyment of the evening, and stressing how much they had been impressed with the natural beauty of the voices. Things were almost back again to the 1912 level — but counter-attractions were to divert the energies of the new generation in the shape of a different fashion in music — the Beat!

During the last few years the quality of Gaelic singing has deteriorated. The vocalists are not so highly trained, and many of the choirs tend to wail rather than sing. The question has been asked, should the choirs adopt guitar accompaniments and prevailing beat?

Personally, in some cases, I should recommend this. We want to get back to the robust Gaelic movement of 1912 — and we must please the vast audience of TV and radio of today. One has only to hear the *Mingulay Boat Song* sung in English by The Galliards to wish it had been sung in Gaelic.

Many Gaelic songs were sung with a defined beat as the accompaniment of natural labour — rowing, waulking the cloth, cutting peats, milking or spinning. One has only to work around this beat to be in line with today's fashion. *'S e ur Beatha* (You're welcome), that delightful TV programme of Gaelic music and song in which the MacDonald sisters from Shader, Lewis, are doing just this, is already proving to be extremely popular, even with non-Gaelic-speaking audiences.

"Suas leis a' Ghàidhlig"*

*Up with Gaelic.

Chapter 17

Fiddlers All

I was sitting listening to those old Gaelic songs, collected by my father and grandmother, coming over the radio — exquisitely sung by Evelyn Campbell and Alasdair Gillies — when it happened. Suddenly I was back in the days of my childhood, when my father and his friends were working in every way possible to save and preserve the Gaelic language, its poetry and its music . . .

Family and friends were, as usual, gathered in our drawing-room, and, as the last notes of the singing died away, the air around me seemed to fill with music — strathspeys and reels, with their genuine flavour in every curve, twist and accent of the bow, as of yore — all executed in perfect taste and steeped in character.

Abruptly the music stopped and a voice inquired, "Did you know I was wanted by the police in Dundee?"

An awed chorus from the audience, "Good gracious, no! Whatever for?"

"To play at their concert next month!"

A mischievous laugh, and on the music went, the bow wielded by an alert, dapper, pawky, kindly little man, in all the glory of tartan, badger sporran, dirk and skean-dhu — a rebellious fringe of grey hair framing his lively face — Scott Skinner!

It was many years later that I learned the story of the little man's life. He was born in Banchory, Kincardineshire, on August 5, 1843, his parents being William (Dancie) Skinner and Mary Agnew. When about six years of age his elder brother, Sandy, taught him to play the fiddle, by ear, and later allowed him to assist him at dances in the district. Later Peter Milne, a first rate fiddler who played at functions up and down Deeside, took him under his wing and gave him much valuable instruction in the correct traditional bowing for Strathspeys and reels.

Three years later Skinner attended Connell's school in Aberdeen, and while there, his brother Sandy took him to a concert given by an orchestra of boys known as "Dr Mark's Little Men". He was so delighted with their performance that he left Aberdeen with them on a six-year apprenticeship. It was during this period that, under the tuition of Charles Rougier, a French violinist, he learned musical theory and became proficient in the playing of classical music.

He was endowed with charm and musical ability, but he was unlucky in love. His first wife, Jane Stuart, assisted him with his dancing classes for about twelve years while they lived in Aberlour — but thereafter, due perhaps to excessive stress and strains, had to spend the rest of her life in Elgin Mental Hospital, her husband living near her in Elgin. When she died, a lonely and sad Skinner made his way back to Aberdeen.

For twelve years after this time he lived near Dundee with his second wife, Dr Gertrude Park, and it was at this time that he composed some of his finest tunes. This marriage, however, did not last, and when Gertrude left him, having rendered him almost penniless with her wild extravagance and then sailed for Rhodesia, it was his staunch friend William MacHardy, laird of Dumblair, Forgue, near Huntly, who came to his assistance, granting him a cottage, rent free, in which to make his home.

By 1917 Skinner's genius was becoming more and more appreciated. In that year at a Burns concert in Edinburgh he was presented with his portrait in oils. The presentation was made by Colonel James Cantlie, R.A.M.C., London, and was unveiled by Mrs Wauchope of Niddrie. Colonel Cantlie maintained "that Scottish music was now more or less wide-spread and was something that would never pass away. Amongst the great composers of national Scottish music three names stood out prominently — Neil Gow, Marshall, and James Scott Skinner. Scotland is their debtor. Let us honour Skinner now on the roll of her national musicians".

Amongst Skinner's works published in book form are *The Miller o' Hin Collection* (1881); *The Elgin Collection* (1884); *The Logie Collection* (1888); *The Scottish Violinist* and *The Harp and Claymore Collection* (1904).

For too long Skinner's reputation has rested on "popular hits" such as *The Bonnie Lass o' Bon Accord*, *The Laird o' Dumblair* and *The Gay Gordons* while gems such as *Huntly Castle*, *Howe o' Echt*,

*Mr A.G. Wilkin's Favourite, The Shakins o' the Pocky, Mr C.T.
Thomson's Fancy, Miss Laura Andrew, The Auld Style's Awa', The
Lodge of Glentanar* and *Marshall's Style* have more or less dis-
appeared into the limbo of forgotten things.

The Strathspey king died in Aberdeen on March 17, 1927. Four
years later a memorial stone was unveiled by his friend Harry
Lauder at his grave in Allanvale Cemetery, Aberdeen.

As often as not, Skinner was accompanied by Alexander Grant,
commonly known among the Gaels as "The Second Scott Skinner". Grant was a wiry, slightly-built man, with finely-cut, weath-
er-beaten features and penetrating blue-grey eyes, all surmounted
by a shock of thick, tawny hair. He was an old-time farmer — a
heavy occupation in these days. Born at Batangorm on Speyside,
he later became tenant of Tomnahurich Farm near Inverness, a
way of life that was neither easy or particularly lucrative. His soul
yearned for something more satisfying, and this he found in fiddle
music and his intense study of wood vibration.

His first venture into the realms of wood vibration was his Spey
fishing rod, for which he was granted the patent. While he held a
secret for the making of those rods, his patent lay in the splices,
which were thicker than the usual, and had a "shoulder" to them.
If the rod had been solid, one would have said these were
swellings. If you cut wood, the weakest point is the splice — and
Grant's splices were so shaped and strengthened that the vibration
and power of the wood was maintained as if it were all of one pice.
The result was a length of cast which surpassed anything previously or since achieved.

As leader of the Strathspey and Reel Society in Inverness, he did
much to popularise this music in its truest form. He usually played
on a violin he'd made himself — being very particular as to just
where and how he fixed the sound post.

I always felt that this man possessed an energy peculiar to
himself, which he was able to transmit. My eldest sister, a Mod
gold medallist, usually played his accompaniments on the piano.
On one occasion, when she was away from home, I was called upon
to take her place. At that time I had never played Highland music,
and I made it quite clear to him that I could do very little to help.

"Just give me a vamp, key a", he said.

I fingered the keys idly.

He gave me a light tap on the head with his bow. "Now we're
off", he chuckled — and we were! Something got into me — and in

complete ignorance of the tunes he was playing, I accompanied his every note. How? I shall never know!

Grant's pet ambition was to invent a violin on his wood vibration principle that would produce truer sound than even a Strad. One night he brought this instrument to our house. The "Body" was round, with "lungs" inside on either side of the sound post. The scroll was rather long, and the bow he used was unusual, for the wood tapered off to its original length, well beyond the tip, thus allowing unbroken vibration. The result was amazing. I have never heard truer notes played on a violin.

Yehudi Menuhin has said, "The violin is the next best to the human voice . . . it's something intimate — nearly part of the body". This *was* the human voice — and an extremely beautiful voice at that — almost out of this world. Unfortunately, Grant died before this instrument was brought to public notice. Today, the Rondello, as he called it, lies more or less in pieces — and so far no one has been found capable of putting it together.

One of our local poets, Bernard George Hoare, wrote the following lines in Grant's memory:

> Master of violins and of the bow
> That sweeps the strings to tuneful melody,
> Player of lively airs and tunes that be
> The genius of your native Strath's outflow,
> With kindred genius nature did bestow
> On you the finer sense of music's round
> And perfect tone; the laws of sound
> Enthralled you, as her child to trace and know.
>
> Craftsman and builder of a truer tone
> Than even the violin now can, mastered, charm;
> Who seeks for perfect finds it not alone,
> Since in the seeking also lies the form.
> You are the silent poet, tuning all the strings
> To perfect interval, where false still rings.

A favourite visitor to our home was Dr Keith Norman Macalister MacDonald. One had only to look at his typically Highland face with its large moustache, the bold nose, the dreamy eyes and high forehead, to say "Skye". And Skye he was — third son of Charles MacDonald, Ord, Sleat, and grandson, on the maternal side, of Captain Neil MacLeod of Gesto.

He was an extremely interesting man. His education, before going to Edinburgh University to study medicine, had been provided by a private tutor in Skye — and it was in Skye that he first practised. From there he went to Lochaber, then North Wales, and finally to India, where he was appointed Civil Surgeon of Prome. It was when in charge of this station that he undertook to translate the practice of medicine among the Burmese from original palmleaf manuscripts which he had procured, after immense trouble, from native doctors. This work he afterwards published, with a historical sketch of the progress of medicine from the earliest times.

Music was his hobby — his violin his best friend. Considered to be one of the most worthy representatives of the leisured amateur class of that day, he had a keen interest in amateur and professional alike. He published a Skye collection of reels and Strathspeys, to which he added some "Fantasias for violin and piano on Scotch and Irish airs". This was highly appreciated. In his famous Gesto Collection of Highland music, published in 1887, he presented many old melodies, which, but for his timely exertions, might have passed away with the older generation, from whose singing and playing he had noted them down. He was also interested in piobaireachd — one of his last works being *Lament for the Mac-Leods of Gesto*.

Not only did he love music but also poetry. His *In Defence of Ossian*, published in 1906, is an unusually scholarly piece of work, whilst his *MacDonald Bards from Medieval Times* (1900), at the end of which he lists and describes ancient Highland dances and their histories, is a mine of information. We felt very sad when, in 1913, we learned of his death in Edinburgh.

In my possession I still have a packet of Dr MacDonald's letters written to my late father during their long friendship. They intrigue me for several reasons. Firstly, there is the notepaper, embellished with a musical score of one of his own compositions. Secondly, there is the keen appreciation of my father's friendship; his warm encouragement for his work, and his glorious enthusiasm for everything associated with Highland music and poetry: "If I were a poet, and could sing, I would sing Highland songs all day long — and far into the night, for there is nothing more beautiful than this in all life".

When I recall fiddlers I have known, my thoughts always come, sooner or later, to Ewen. He was our gardener — a worthy character of the old school, if ever there was one, who spoke to the flowers in Gaelic, because "they understand it better than the

English". In his early years he had been a coachman: "A gran' life, Miss Mairi — sitting up yonder in my fine coat and top hat, the lovely horses in front of me, and the bonnie leddies behind. What more could a man ask for?" What, indeed!

For some reason best known to himself, Ewen always arrived wearing a black tail coat and sporting a "dickie", which, after a few minutes' work, usually got out of hand — and waistcoat! Ewen was a "lad o' pairts". He would sit down on a chair, and, straightening his "dickie", take out his fiddle, which he always brought with him, and launch into a tune. Reels, Strathspeys and jigs followed each other with just that unique "kick" that made one's feet beat out the rhythm.

"There's nothing like a tune to lift the weariness from the bones", he would say. "You just forget all your bothers — an' feel a new person. Music's a wonderful tonic — it gets you above yourself".

Suddenly I understood the importance of the tail coat and "dickie"!

Several years later I learned that Ewen had been found dead, in his humble lodgings, dressed as of yore in his tail coat and "dickie" — his beloved fiddle by his side.

It had always been a bitter disappointment to Scott Skinner that Manson, the son of his first marriage, though an excellent dancer, had no interest whatsoever in the fiddle or fiddle music. Actually, Manson left Britain and settled in Australia.

He served with the Anzacs in the First World War, and afterwards returned there for good. Skinner used to wonder who would carry on his work after his day was done. Would it all be forgotten and lost for ever?

He need not have worried. In recent years fiddle music has become more and more popular, the popularity of "The Fiddler's Rally" at the Mod being proof of this fact. Skinner's work never died; his music today is in as great demand as ever it was, if not more so. All over the country, Strathspey and reel societies are flourishing — not least of all in Inverness, where Skinner and Grant still seem to preside over the players as they delight enthusiastic audiences.

Chapter 18

The Enigma of Gordon Daviot

GORDON Daviot died in 1952, and the feeling of loss which her passing meant to Scottish literature has increased, rather than diminished. Particularly is this so in Inverness, where those interested in drama found in her a townswoman whose knowledge of the theatre was invaluable, and whose original plays were a delight to act.

Strange as it may seem, few of us had ever known the real person. We had rubbed shoulders with her in our busy streets; admired her pretty home and picturesque garden — and some had even shared schooldays with her — yet no one enjoyed her companionship, for Gordon Daviot was, and wished to be what she herself termed herself, "a lone wolf", discouraging any attempts at fraternisation, and turning aside from the social life to which her genius allowed her ready entry. Such friendships as she enjoyed were those of people of creative ability — authors, actors, actresses and the like — and these found her eager to respond to all they had to offer. It is in her work that we find the real Gordon Daviot, and there we learn to know her intimately.

As a schoolgirl Gordon is remembered as a happy, very active young person, trim in her sailor suit with its braided collar; her light brown hair always smoothly brushed — and ever ready to break into a most attractive, lively smile. Lessons for her proved more or less unattractive — her one delight being to escape from the rigours and dullness of the schoolroom, and scamper off to the cloakroom, where, upon an old set off parallel bars — housed there for no apparent reason — she delighted herself and others by turning somersaults, and performing various other acrobatics in a highly expert manner.

In "The Daughter of Time", we recognise in the nurse the schoolgirl who wrote on her title pages:

Elizabeth MacKintosh,
      Class II,
   Inverness Royal Academy,
      Inverness,
         Inverness-shire,
            Scotland,
               Europe,
                  The World,
                     The Universe.

and who embellished this effort with designs of "scraps". We recognise, too, the little girl who played "noughts and crosses" with her neighbour, drew moustaches and spectacles on the portraits of the Kings of Scotland — and sometimes even on their Queens, and "doodled" the dreary hours away as best she could, until the glorious moment of freedom. Yes — that was a young person known affectionately to her school chums as "Bessie MacK".

In her "thriller", "Miss Pym Disposes", we are introduced to the next period of her life, for in the plot of this story we find her experiences while training at a Physical Training College in Birmingham. Her early love of the parallel bars was no desultory caprice — it had remained with her and decided her life's profession.

One is tempted to inquire, sometimes, why this young woman, trained as a physical training instructress, and holding posts near Liverpool and in Tunbridge Wells, should suddenly turn authoress and playwright. Actually there was nothing sudden about the change of vocation, for while engaged in her profession, her hobby was the pen, and several short stories were published by her in "The English Review". Then came "Kif", her first novel, to be followed by a clever detective story, "The Man in The Queue", written under the pseudonym "Gordon Daviot" — and this name began to attract attention as that of a promising new writer.

Of her first play, "Richard of Bordeaux", produced in London in 1932, conflicting stories have circulated. Some insisted that it was the fruit of her English classes when at Oxford — but as she had never been to Oxford this was obviously false. Others mentioned Froissart but failed to divulge just what Froissart had contributed to the work.

Personally, I have always felt that the entirely new light her plot shed on the character of Richard was something which grew from a

tiny seed sown early in her fertile mind by a master of The
Inverness Royal Academy. Just before the first World War this
school had the advantage of an English Master, who, himself a
graduate of Oxford University, had enjoyed an exceedingly generous education — and this, coupled with an original and highly
cultured mind, produced a person who delighted his classes by his
intimate knowledge of Shakespeare. Many were the hours spent in
discussion as to why Hamlet had obeyed a particular impulse
under certain emotions; whether Shylock was just a typical Jew or
an everyday userer indigenous to any nation, or whether Richard
II was indeed "lily-livered" or what was now termed "pacifist",
and if "pacifist", a great, rather than a weak character.

There is just a possibility that this picture of Richard caught her
very lively imagination, and that, over the years — years during
which pacifism became a burning topic, owing to war, the characters developed and attained the stature which they enjoy in the
play. This, coupled with a puckish, sarcastic wit, produced a play
for which leading actors were asking — good historical background — yet light enough to be entertaining, and a play which
would allow of almost glamorous decor.

It was Sir John Gielgud who first saw possibilities in this play.
Certain parts of the work had to be altered, re-written, almost
recast — and Gordon Daviot proved more than ready to comply.
Grateful for criticism, and ready to accept advice, she at once
established her genius, for, to her, it was the play that mattered,
and to make it successful, no work was too arduous. Painstaking
and accurate in all her research, she eventually produced a play
which was wellnigh perfect, and which adapted itself to the theatre
of its day as few other modern plays have done. That the work of
Sir John Gielgud, who took the part of Richard, and himself
produced the play, was absolutely magnificent, and gave the play a
setting and splendour which could not have been given by any
other can never be denied, and Gordon Daviot was always more
than ready to admit her "luck" in having her work handled by one
of such ability and genius.

For any person to attain to sudden fame from the obscurity of
ordinary life must be something of an ordeal — and so it was to
Gordon Daviot. Inundated with social invitations; laudation from
the press; laudation from all interested in the theatre and the arts;
discussed in her home-town; discussed in London, what were her
reactions?

It was here that general opinion found itself puzzled and dismayed, for it completely failed to understand and assess this rather shy, very simple young woman. In her own life she was happy — but she had a serious urge — the urge to create and continue to create new characters; to produce more plays; to write more novels — and always the fear was that her time to do these things might prove too short.

This time urge was almost an obsession. "If there's anything you want to do, do it now. We shall all be in little boxes soon enough", was one of her favourite pieces of advice. Fired with this urge she found it necessary to discourage those who now clamoured for her friendship. Her puckish sarcasm was her weapon, and she used it ruthlessly. On one occasion, when asked by the Rector of The Academy whether she could mention anything acquired during her schooldays which had proved helpful in her career, she replied with a bright smile — "Oh, I have no doubt whatsoever that the four-leaved clovers I so often found at interval-time, in the playground, were responsible for my great good luck". It was not easy to further conversation in this vein, and eventually her repartee produced the desired effect, and she was left unmolested, to proceed with her work.

At this juncture the deep simplicity of her character asserted itself positively. Having retired from her physical training profession, as housekeeper to her aged father she blithely undertook her full share of all household duties, more or less working to a timetable which suited her dual purpose, allowing plenty of leisure for her beloved hobby.

Her next play, "The Laughing Woman", was based on the life of a recently dead sculptor, Henri Daudier. It was a love story, but though its production was outstanding for the fine, sensitive performance of Stephen Haggard, the play failed to attract, I think, more on account of its very drab setting than for any real fault in plot construction.

Two months later came "Queen of Scots", also produced by Sir John Gielgud, with Miss Gwen Ffrangcon-Davies as the leading lady. This play, although running for over a hundred performances, failed to fulfil expectations, and Sir John Gielgud suggested it disappointed because it avoided the important issue of the Casket Letters. I should rather say, however, that here again the setting was too drab to satisfy. Where were such court scenes, such beautiful gowns and colourful personalities as had given life and

lustre to "Richard of Bordeaux?" True, we could not expect just
such specular magnificence in Scotland — but need every act have
been set in those dreary, bare, dull surroundings?

From a fairly early age she had made a study of calligraphy, and
claimed that it was always possible to read character from hand-
writing. It is, therefore, interesting, at this point to read what she
herself wrote about "Queen of Scots" in a letter to Elizabeth Kyle,
the well-known authoress, who, also, has an Inverness connection.

"If I had seen Bothwell's handwriting before I wrote 'Queen of
Scots', by the way, I would have made him a very different man.
The handwriting is a shock. Educated, clear-minded, construc-
tive, controlled. The complete opposite of the man that we have
been led to believe in. More like Claverhouse's than anyone else's
that I can think of. And handwriting doesn't lie. Apart for one's
walk it is the only thing from the cradle to the grave that we make
entirely out of our own predilections and peculiarities. The complete giveaway! Oh, that mine enemy would write a book, is
redundant. It is sufficient for one's enemy to write some words
with a pen!"

It was not until 1947 that "The Little Dry Thorn" appeared at
The Lyric Theatre, Hammersmith. This play, based upon the
Biblical story of Abraham and Sara, was written in contemporary
colloquial language — a departure which Gordon Daviot favoured
with great success in many of her works. It emphasised the faith of
Abraham — a part finely spoken and magnificently acted by
Henry Ainley — and the loving devotion of Sara, in which part
Angela Baddeley gave a marvellous performance.

Here again we glimpse the real person, for Gordon Daviot was a
diligent and enlightened student of The Bible and Biblical history
— and although a rare church-goer, could expound and explain
the Gospel far more intimately than many who wag their heads in
pulpits. This play failed, however, on account of its lack of
dramatic appeal.

The following year "Valerius" was produced in the Saville
Theatre, London. This was the story of a Roman commander's
struggle to maintain a fort on Hadrian's wall — and though
excellently written lacked an inner conflict, which proved its
undoing.

A year later "The Stars Bow Down" — a play concerned with
Joseph's rise to power in Egypt, showed a return to the more

vigorous style of her earlier plays, but even so failed to hold the public as "Richard of Bordeaux" had done.

"Leith Sands and Other Short Plays" published in 1946, contains some first-class writing. Two of these plays are Biblical, three modern, and the rest historical. In the title play the playwright brings to our notice one of her pet hobbies — for the play is a study of mob psychology, and Gordon Daviot was a keen student of psychology. In one of her "thrillers", "The Franchise Affair" — an eighteenth century "cause célèbre" brought up to date, and put in modern dress — the plot centres round the unexpected reactions of a youthful female mind to certain conditions.

Since she was endowed with extraordinarily keen perception, research was for her a joy — and it was this quality in her make-up that led to her aptitude for writing thrillers. These include, "The Daughter of Time", "To Love and Be Wise", "Brat Farrar", "The Franchise Affair", "Miss Pym Disposes", "A Shilling for Candles", "The Man in the Queue", and "The Singing Sands", and most of them feature as their hero, Grant, a Scottish-born inspector from Scotland Yard. In these she freely uses her unusual gift of discernment to weave plots which enthral the reader. Psychology, study of hand-writing, historical research, the cogency of vanity and ambition are all employed, and in each we find that trenchant wit which was so much a trait of the authoress herself.

Her serious works, "The Expensive Halo", "Kif", "Life of Claverhouse", and "The Privateer", exhibit the same formula. The two former are well considered psychological studies of modern life, whilst the two latter are outstanding for their research. In "Life of Claverhouse" the historical research required covers more or less "home territory" — but "The Privateer" is remarkable for research whose locus is foreign territory, never even visited by the authoress.

"The Privateer" is a cleverly written tale of a Welshman, Henry Morgan, who, turning privateer, wins a series of almost bloodless engagements against the Spaniards on different islands in the Caribbean Sea, eventually being appointed Lieutenant-Governor of Jamaica. So correct is every minute detail of scenery — and scenery of that especial period; so real is the atmosphere of sailors, buccaneers, sailing ships, the language of seafarers and their habits, that the story might well have been written by Henry Morgan himself, and merely translated into more modern composition.

In spite of her able wit and quick repartee Gordon Daviot suffered from a certain shyness — an unwillingness to meet strangers which was almost pathological in its intensity. She was known to admit that when conversing with Londoners she found she had to "translate mentally" in order to be completely lucid, for her expressions seemed to convey a rather different shade of meaning from those of her companions, and she gave it as her opinion that hers was a difficulty common to all Scots. Here again her keen perception manifests itself, for although, in composition, her English was carefully chosen and faultless, and likewise, in conversation, she could attain brilliance, she was apt, on occasion, to lapse into the Inverness idiom — a form which may succeed in expressing something totally different from what is understood outside Scotland.

A short story will illustrate how devastating this can be. An Inverness lady, wishing to impress a Londoner with her musical ability remarked, "Of course, I was on the piano for years". To her astonishment the Englishman replied, "How d——d uncomfortable you must have been". This "mental shyness" coupled with a preference for the elderly rather than for those of her own age, tended to make her shun rather than seek society. She often asserted with a quick smile — "I won't go to anyone's house until they're bedridden. Then I'll go and see them as often as they like" — and she did, showing a kindness, thoughtfulness, and tenderness which surprised many of her contemporaries.

Yet she did appreciate youthful friendship of one particular kind, and that was when, after "Richard of Bordeaux" had run for a whole year and the cast had been supplied with new costumes, some of their number made a patchwork cushion from small squares of the original costumes, and sent it to her with beautiful bouquets of flowers, as a token of their esteem and enjoyment of her play. Never was she so excited — and she treasured that cushion all her life.

She enjoyed the good things of this world — clothes, good food and wine, horse-racing — and the cinema. A sincere lover of the country, she had a horror of living long in the city. Unusually quick-minded she could finish writing a thriller in about six weeks — though a work necessitating research required much more preparation. Self-pity was to her the unpardonable sin, and anything in the nature of "whine" she scorned.

Her original pseudonym, Gordon Daviot, under which she

published all her plays and serious works was chosen from the picturesque district of Daviot, near Inverness, where she and her family spent happy holidays together in their youth.

For her "thrillers", however, she adopted the nom-de-plume of Josephine Tey — Josephine having been her mother's name, and Tey the surname of her English grandmother — and it is this pseudonym that enlightens regarding the most surprising trait of her character — for Gordon Daviot, although born and bred in the Highlands of Scotland, and bearing the grand Highland surname of MacKintosh, loved England with all her heart and soul. Scotland, to her, was pictureseque — beautiful, but its people were inefficient, inarticulate, vacillating, and narrow-minded. It amused her, as did its highly inadequate Gaelic tongue which had never troubled to add an extra word to its vocabulary for over two hundred years, and contented itself with a "Gaelicising" of the modern English term — but it failed to intrigue. Her English blood flowed strongly in her veins — and to her, as she so beautifully expressed this feeling through the medium of Henry Morgan in "The Privateer", England was "home". Returning to London, he found—

"It was summertime, the beginning of July. And before his eyes as the coach made its slow way up to London was trailed the green, wild-rose loveliness of England. He had never seen it before: this ultimate loveliness of nature; and he sat enchanted . . . But when Englishmen said 'home', this was what they meant; this incredible perfection.

"He tried to think of something that might challenge its incomparability; the liquid light of Caribbean Seas, the flaming blossoms in the dust, the savanna grass, the jungle prodigality. But all those were lovely details in a picture; here the whole picture was composed of lovely details, fresh and jewelled as an illuminated letter. He sat and watched it, hour after hour. England. This was what men meant when they said England".

It is not surprising, therefore, to learn that it was to England she journeyed to die. Her innate stoicism which scorned "whine" refused to admit ill-heath, and none of her friends even suspected her secret. She had often gone south for a holiday — and when she announced her intention of "going south for Xmas" her decision was accepted without question. Her last novel in print, she had won her race against time, and could well afford to lay her pen aside, satisfied that she had fulfilled her mission.

Elizabeth Kyle attended her funeral, and I now quote from the letter she sent me afterwards:—

"You ask about the funeral. James Bridie's wife was there and spoke to me. She said Gordon had always got on so well with her husband, that she felt she wanted to come to represent them both, though, of course, he was then dead. John Gielgud, also, and Edith Evans. I did not recognise anyone else. But I couldn't bear the sight of the 'little box' she had so often spoken of, sliding quietly into a hole in the wall without one flower on it."

This would have been in accordance with her own wishes, and probably, even, her strict injunctions, for she loathed the panoply of mourning, considered its rites a barbaric survival, and had a strong personal dislike to flowers on graves. She was cremated at Streatham Crematorium, the service being attended by a number of her theatre friends, who were anxious to pay their last respects to one whom they had all genuinely adored.

To England, too, apart from a few personal bequests, she bequeathed practically all of her considerable fortune. In her last will and testament she instructed that everything she possessed, whether money, goods, property, personal possessions, investments, play, book, and film rights and royalties, and any other belongings, be devoted to furthering the work of The National Trust for England. Her estate was valued at £26,718, and she further instructed that if the sum accruing to the Trust were large enough, it should be known as the Daviot Fund, and used for some specific purpose; and not added anonymously to the general assets of the Trust.

To the Inverness Museum she left an early Victorian gold ring set with emeralds and diamonds, which she had worn for the greater part of her life; the original script of "Richard of Bordeaux", and a collection of tartans and silver spoons which she had previously lent to the musuem.

. . . As the years roll on we shall remember her and bless her memory, grateful in heart for the many happy hours her work afforded us — and proud to recall that she was a citizen of our Highland Capital.

Chapter 19

The Seven Men

FOLLOWING the defeat of Prince Charlie at Culloden and the removal of the Duke of Cumberland to Fort Augustus, sad days fell upon the people of Glenmoriston. On Cumberland's instructions, soldiers, like so many packs of hounds, were sent into the glen to spread terror and destruction. These troops ravaged the glen from end to end, shooting down men, burning their homesteads, subjecting maids and matrons to the grossest brutality, and driving to their fort every four-footed animal they could find.

Goaded into fury by this treatment, seven men — six of them of the glen — strong of physique and of indomitable will, banded together and resolved, as far as lay in their power, to make the lives of the invaders dangerous and uncertain. Their determination was sharpened, and their anger and disgust knew no bounds, on learning that Ludovic Grant of Grant, having persuaded certain men of Glenurquhart and Glenmoriston to travel to Inverness and give up their arms on the promise of a free pardon, had not raised a finger when these men were seized by the Hanoverian troops and carried off for deportation as slaves to Jamaica.

Some little distance from Glenmoriston was the wild inaccessible district of Coire Dho — where the natives had had their summer shielings, or cattle grazings, from time immemorial. To this remote spot, buried in the heart of the hills, many of the glen people had fled, in the hope of escaping the doom meted out to so many of their friends and relatives. The River Doe flows through the entire corrie, its tributaries dividing the land up into smaller corries. Two of these are Coire Mheadhain — the centre corrie — and Coire Sgrainge — the gloomy corrie.

It was in Coire Dho that the seven men made their headquarters. All but one had served in the Prince's army until Culloden, and now bound themselves by solemn oath of offence and defence against Cumberland and his troops, "never to yield, but to die on the spot; never to give up their arms for all the days of their lives".

Ill-informed writers have often alluded to these gallant men as "robbers", "caterans" or "thieves". No descriptions could be further from the truth. They were, without exception, honest tacksmen — men who held land on lease from the superior — or farmers. Their names were:—

1 — Patrick Grant, tenant of Craskie — the leader.

2 — John Macdonald, also of Craskie.

3 — Alexander MacDonald, tacksman of Aonach (my ancestor).

4, 5 and 6 — Alexander, Donald, and Hugh Chisholm, sons of Paul Chisholm, tenant of Blairie.

7 — Grigor MacGregor* — probably not a native of Glenmoriston — a deserter from Loudon's regiment, who had joined the Jacobite force in the Corrieyairack.

At this point a short history of the family of MacDonald of Aonach is of interest. Until practically the end of the fifteenth century Glenmoriston was included in the princely dominions of the MacDonalds, Lords of the Isles, and was held for them by Mac Iain Ruaidh (Son of Red John), a vassal chief, and a cadet of those MacDonalds. Annually, at the Inn at Aonach, Macianruaidh met the Lord of the Isles and they exchanged shirts, which ceremony constituted Mac Iain Ruaidh his "Léine-chrios" — fast friend. It amounted to an oath of fidelity.

When King James IV found it necessary to curtail the power of such insular potentates, these MacDonalds were deprived of most of their lands, which were eventually transferred to Sir Duncan Grant of Freuchy, for his loyalty to the crown. He handed them to his grandson, John Grant. "Am Bard Rhuadh" — the Red haired Bard — who handed them to John, his natural son, who was the first laird of Grant to take up residence in Glenmoriston. MacDonald of Aonach was descended from the MacDonalds who originally owned Glenmoriston.

From Coire Dho the Seven Men engaged in guerilla warfare against the devastators of their country, making the Whig Highlanders, who accompanied the Hanoverian soldiers as guides, their especial targets.

---

* The late Bruce Lockhart was proud to claim this man as an ancestor.

About the beginning of July 1746, the two MacDonalds and the Chisholms caught sight of a party of seven redcoats, guided by Archibald MacPherson, a native of Skye, travelling from Fort Augustus to Glenelg with two horses laden with wine, wheaten bread and other provisions. They fired from behind some boulders, killing two of the soldiers. Alarmed, the remainder of the party fled, leaving horses and provisions to the attackers.

Some days later the Seven Men met Robert Grant, a native of Strathspey at Feith Rob, and shot him through the heart. Cutting off his head, they fixed it in a tree near the high road at Blairie, as a warning to all who helped the redcoats.

On hearing that cattle, belonging to Patrick Grant's uncle had been seized by Hanoverian soldiers, and were being driven off towards the West Coast, they gave chase, and after several forays eventually caught the soldiers in a narrow pass and drove the cattle and a horse laden with provisions back to Coire Dho.

Meanwhile Prince Charlie and his party, consisting of Major MacDonald of Glenaladale, Lieutenant John MacDonald, his brother, and Lieutenant John MacDonald of Borrodale, had arrived at Loch Hourn, intended to make for Glenshiel in Seaforth's country, having heard that some French vessels were cruising in Loch Ewe, and being hopeful that the Prince might make his escape to the Continent in one of them. For this journey they needed a guide and provisions.

When Glenaladale was discussing the project with his friends, a lad was seen approaching them whose face seemed familiar to him. When questioned the lad said he was Donald MacDonald, a native of Glengarry; he had served in the Prince's army, and was fleeing from soldiers who had killed his father the previous day. Glenaladale chose him as guide. Meanwhile, two scouts returned with butter and cheese, the only food they could find, and as young Borrodale later reported, "Words cannot express the quantity we consumed, though both were exceeding salt".

Some hours later Glenaladale received the depressing news that the only French ship that had been in Loch Ewe had sailed — and immediately it was decided to travel northwards. Eventually they all climbed a hill above Strath Cluanie, where they lay concealed all day in the heather. Hearing sounds of enemy firing, however, when dark fell they decided to move on.

Taking a sharp turn north they reached the summit of Sgur nan Conbhairean from where, at early dawn — after a most miserable

His line came from
ALASDAIR CUTACH
(Short Alastair. A famous hunter)
|
JOHN
|
ALASDAIR BUIDHE
*(Fair-haired Alastair MacDonald of Aonach — one of
The Seven Men)*
|
CHARLES
(Born when the Prince was in the cave)
|
JOHN   MALCOLM   DONALD
|
ANGUS
|
ALEXANDER
(My father)

night spent in an open cave, tormented by midges, with neither
room to stand upright nor lie down, and no fuel for a fire to dry out
their wet clothes — they found themselves looking down into
Coire Dho. It was resolved that Glenaladale's brother and the
Glengarry lad should be sent to ask whether any of the Seven Men,
with whose exploits they were familiar, would be willing to act as
guide to a fugitive Jacobite gentleman.

In due course the emissaries returned, saying that they had
found three of The Men in the corrie, and that these had told them
to bring the gentleman — who they thought was young Clanranald
— to the corrie. Charles and his friends then set out for this
stronghold, and were met before arrival by MacDonald of
Aonach, John MacDonald, and Alexander Chisholm.

To appreciate what actually took place here — for there has
been much controversy about there having been two caves in
which the Prince was hid — one must fully understand the
meaning of the Gaelic term "uamh". The translation of this word
is "a cave" or "a den". It was in Coire Sgrainge that Rory the
Hunter hid his cattle, where there was concealed a "den" flanked
by a dense wood. It was to this "den" that The Men first took the
Prince, to await the return — from a foraging expedition — of the
rest of their party.

Lockhart Bogle has painted a very well-known picture of
"Prince Charles in the cave at Coire Dho" — but he is far from
correct in depicting the Prince as he does. Suffering from dysen-
tery and fatigue, he must have been barely recognisable; bare-

footed, wearing an old black kilt tunic, dirty shirt, nondescript waistcoat and short kilt, his head covered by an unsavoury "barran"* which hung down under his bonnet to defy the midges whose bites had swollen and inflamed his face; his red beard long and unkempt; a gun in his hand and pistol and dirk by his side. He cut an extremely odd figure — but The Men, doffing their bonnets, showed they knew who the Jacobite gentleman was.

*A kerchief often tied round the forehead to relieve headache. In this case, however, the "barran" was an old, rather dirty linen night-cap.

Leading the newcomers to a very sheltered part of the corrie they produced mutton, butter, cheese, and whisky, all of which was much enjoyed by the Prince who had had no food for forty-eight hours. Next The Men hid their guest in a deep bed of heather, and within seconds he was fast asleep, The Men hiding themselves nearby in the heather to keep guard.

On awakening, the Prince indicated that he did not wish to increase the number of his bodyguard, and suggested that the MacDonalds and Chisholms should take them to a safer place, without waiting for the return of their companions. This The Men refused to do, explaining that they were bound by solemn oath to stand together. Charles did not press the matter further, but asked them to swear to fidelity and secrecy — a request they readily granted.

Glenaladale then administered the following oath—

> That their backs should be to God and their faces to the Devil, and that all the curses the Scriptures did pronounce might come upon them and all their posterity if they did not stand firm by the Prince in the greatest dangers, and if they did discover to any person — man, woman, or child, that the Prince was in their keeping, till once this person should be out of danger.

This obligation was so carefully adhered to that it was fully a year after Charles was safely back in France before anyone knew that the Prince had been hidden by the Seven Men.

Charles and Glenaladale offered to swear "That if danger should come upon them they should stand by one another to the last drop of their blood". The Men refused to accept this oath, insisting that in ultimate danger Charles was to save himself, any way he could, and leave them to their fate.

Next day the foraging party of The Men returned with a live ox and a dead deer — and readily took the same oath as their companions had done. Then one of The Men went to Fort Augustus, where he procured bread, and "dainty of dainties", a pennyworth of gingerbread. For three days the Prince rested in this corrie, and was "so well refreshed that he thought himself able to encounter any hardships".

On August 2 the whole party went to Rory's cave in Coire-Mheadhain, now know as the "Prince's Cave", where they hid for a further four days. It was during this period that The Men got to know Charles really intimately, and found him to be of an extremely cheerful, pleasant disposition, kindly and friendly in his manner, and completely undismayed by hardships.

Once settled in the cave the Prince — using Borrodale as interpreter — told them that he had great confidence in the King of France as a true and fast friend, and that his father and his brother Henry would risk their all to save him. He addressed The Men as his Privy Council — the first he had had since Culloden — and allowed them to call him Dugald MacCullony — Son of the Servant of the Lord.

He asked them to refrain from removing their bonnets when in his presence, as he was now "one of themselves". All sat in a circle when eating, each having his particular share on his knee, the Prince proving to have an excellent appetite. He loved to assist with the cooking, often roasting the meat and showing the others how to cook it more tastily, as he helped himself to a piece off the spit, and munched it while waiting for the whole to be fully cooked.

Sometimes he was in a romantic mood and told The Men about his sweetheart — one of the daughters of the King of France. Her hair was black as the raven, and she was a mighty fine, agreeable lady, sweet-tempered and humble. He couldn't help loving her, and felt she had a great regard for him, as had the Dauphin, whom he praised warmly.

John MacDonald — the pawky member of his audience — on one occasion remarked, "Seeing the lady is so 'cannach'* it's a pity she's not here now. We'd be very kind to her and take great care of her". This caused merriment all round, the Prince answering, "God forbid, for were she here and seized, to ransom her person would make peace all over Europe upon any terms the Elector of Hanover would propose".

Upon rising in the morning Charles never failed to say his

*Pleasing

prayers, and during his association with The Men prevailed upon them to give up swearing.

These halcyon days were abruptly brought to an end when news arrived that the Black Campbell of Kintail, who commanded a company of the Ross-shire militia, was raiding the country and lifting all the cattle he could lay hands on near a camp he had set up, less than four miles from the cave. With one accord it was decided to "up sticks" and make for Strath Glass, the territory of the friendly Chisholms.

Leaving Aonach and Alexander Chisholm behind to watch the movements of Campbell, the rest set off, travelling by rough mountain paths known only to The Men, arriving at early dawn in Strath Glass, where they hid until evening, when Aonach and Chisholm joined them, assuring them they need have no fear of Campbell for the moment.

For rather more than three weeks The Men, hunted from place to place by the enemy, travelled with the Prince, until they saw him safely delivered into the friendly hands of Lochiel and Dr Cameron. Partings were sad as Charles bade farewell to the faithful Glenaladale and The Men, promising fervently never to forget them should he come into his own.

Lastly he bade farewell to Patrick Grant, who he had insisted should remain with him until money was available for each member of the party. When this was arranged, he gave Patrick twenty-four guineas, being three guineas for each of the seven men and for Hugh MacMillan who had joined them when on their way to Strath Glass. Patrick then returned to Glenmoriston to share the money with his friends.

Before leaving the cave the Prince had given Aonach a powder-horn. This powder-horn, black with a white bone top, enjoys an honoured place in our hall today.

When Aonach went to the cave, before the arrival of the Prince, he took a three-legged pot with him from his own home, and some other small utensils. After the Hanoverian troops had left the district, he carried the pot home again, and also a small wooden cuach† from which the Prince had drunk his whisky. This is also in our possession.

The pot was handed down in my father's family, eventually

†A drinking cup.

becoming the property of his aunt, who had always promised that he should have it "after her day".

Things did not, however, work out that way. With advancing years the old lady became very confused, and Ian Robert I. Murray Grant of Glenmoriston, fearing the pot might be lost, and desirous of preserving it for all time for Glenmoriston, persuaded her to sell it for a small consideration, to him. It is now, therefore, a Grant heirloom.

Chapter 20

In Search of MacIan

THOUGH MacIan's prints, or copies of the originals, are popular throughout Britain today, very little is known about MacIan himself. No known portrait of him exists, but I hope to suggest later in this article that a likeness may be found, painted by no less a person than the artist's wife.

I have always loved MacIan's works, and had inquired of numerous libraries and art galleries for details of his life. The replies were all disappointing — save one, which told me that in some records he was referred to as Robert Roland MacIan; in others as Robert Ronald MacIan or McIan — and that he had been born in Inverness in 1803.

The fact that I could claim his as a townsman made me determined to continue my search, and eventually I learned that his ancestors had belonged to the MacIans of Glencoe. As a young man, he had left Inverness and travelled to London, where he became an actor.

I could very well understand his going to London, for at this time Scotland's music, art, and a way of life were making a remarkable impact on Londoners — introduced to them by the Highland Society of London, under the patronage of most of the leading Highland chiefs of the day. It was, for a man of his genius, a very logical decision. But why had he gone on the stage? What kind of parts did he play? What sort of life had he lived in London? Who had been his friends? Nowhere could I find an answer to my questions — so for a time I had to give up the quest.

My father, during his lifetime, had built up a library, including every conceivable book and pamphlet about Inverness. Often I will pick out an odd volume and ramble through its pages — losing myself in the past. In that frame of mind, I picked out, one evening lately, a small volume of poems — *The Mountain Heath* whose author was an Invernessian — David MacDonald. Idly I began to read. He'd obviously been a baker:

"Mould up the English, French, and Cundum Rolls,
And Sandwiches and Turnovers, with holes;
And Coburg Loaves and Cottages and Twists—
All made of Wights, and fashioned with the fists . . .
Waking, baking, making bread;
Pitching, crouching, bitching trade!"

Soon I felt I liked David, and his unconventional rhymes, and I continued to read. Then I sat up with a start. Before my eyes were the words — "To R. R. MacIan, Esq." As I read on I realised that David MacDonald and MacIan had been close friends.

My first reaction to this discovery was to try to find out something more about David MacDonald. An old Inverness pamphlet (1863) confirmed that he had been a baker, and had gone to London where he had carried on his trade for many years — until from overwork he developed consumption, and returned to Inverness in 1836, where he died a few years later.

On the margin of the pamphlet, in my father's handwriting, were the words "See *Clan Donald Journal* Nov. 1896." I expected to find something more about David here, but to my amazement what I found was a letter begging that something be done about cataloguing the works of MacIan, and writing up his life's story. The writer mentioned that MacIan was known to be an expert swordsman, and added that he had painted as a commission a picture of the action of Stone Ferry in the American War of Independence, where a party of two hundred recruits of the Fraser Highlanders successfully withstood two thousand of the enemy for several hours. In this picture, he noted, "the piper continues to play seated beside a wounded officer. The swordsmanship of the various figures is excellent, and the forest background effective."

Feeling like Sherlock Holmes at his best, I again took up *The Mountain Heath*. Right away one verse from David MacDonald's pen gave me MacIan's correct name:

"But of myself I need not speak,
I am, Clansman Ronald,
Thine ever ready, at command,
Yours faithfully, MacDonald."

I now knew beyond any real doubt that his name was Robert Ronald MacIan.

Continuing to read MacDonald's poems, I found that MacIan was in the habit of giving him complimentary tickets for the plays in which he acted, and these, along with a lady friend, MacDonald joyfully attended. On the following page I found *The Combat*, with a note to the effect that this "combat" occurred in the play entitled *The Covenanters* which was acted in the English Opera House, London, in 1835 — and here was MacIan on the stage along with another actor of the name of Wilson, engaged in a duelling exhibition.

> "Nor sooner did the pipes their pealings sound
> Than those brave men towards each other bound;
> They close and for the fatal thrust contend,
> Yet equally were skilful to defend.
> Sword to sword their eyes determin'd fixed,
> They paus'd, while every vein were strain'd and rax'd;
> Keen, desperate the contest seem'd the while,
> Blow parried blow, yet neither would recoil.
> They turn, they twist, they stretch, they strive, they strain—
> Nor yet one inch could on each other gain.
>
> Fierce was the combat fought on either side,
> Wild as the blast that ocean's waves divide."

Now I knew why MacIan had gone on the stage. His expert swordsmanship had won him a place.

John Wilson, I found, had been born in Edinburgh in 1800. He had a beautiful tenor voice, and sang a leading part in opera in the Covent Garden Theatre. Owing to the financial failures of several London theatres, he gave up opera and became an entertainer, illustrating Scottish life and music. A report of his having given three musical entertainments the previous week appears in *The Inverness Courier* of October 7, 1840. These evenings were very much enjoyed by the townsfolk. He eventually went to the United States, where he became tremendously popular.

David MacDonald's next poem told me that MacIan, too, was a singer — and also that he had been a member of The Club of True Highlanders:

> "My dear MacIan, on this night
> The 'Comunn Gael' meet,
> Within the British Coffee-house
> That stands in Cockspur Street.
> And by the Dougal Creature's ghost
> I hope to see you there,
> That you may give a Highland song
> If you have one to spare."

The Club of True Highlanders in London, founded between

1815 and 1816, was an off-shoot of that started in 1815 by Colonel MacDonell of Glengarry, at Inverlochy. The club advertised itself as having been formed to perpetuate the language, dress, music, and characteristics of the Highlander, and its functions attracted many erudite and interesting Gaels. All its members spoke Gaelic.

The club encouraged Highland sports, too, and David gives us a picture of a shinty match in which MacIan played, on Blackheath Common in 1836.

Turning another page I was introduced to James Logan, whose historical account accompanied MacIan's drawings in *The Clans of the Scottish Highlands*,* published in 1845. Logan was born in Aberdeen about 1794, and entered Marischal College to study law. While there, however, he suffered a severe accident to his head — so severe indeed that it proved almost fatal, and he had to give up his law studies. When partially recovered, under the patronage of Lord Aberdeen, he took up art, and became a student at the Royal Academy. One has only to compare his stodgy figures of Highlanders with the picturesque, almost stage-like supple elegance of those of MacIan to realise that Logan was wise to give up art and take to the pen.

Lastly, I met Fanny — Fionghal MacIan — MacIan's wife. "Blithe and bonny, sweet as honey." That was all MacDonald told me about her. From other sources, however, I learned that Fanny was for a long time a mistress — some authorities say headmistress — in the Female School of Design at Somerset House, which at that time housed also the Royal Academy.

I found that Fanny had exhibited at least one picture, "Portraits of the Red Star of the Evening and the Diving Mouse, the wife and sister of the Chippewa Chief, Makcoonce" at the Royal Academy in 1836. Between 1835 and 1837, while still an actor, MacIan exhibited paintings at Suffolk Street and in 1836 exhibited at the Royal Academy for the first time. I think, therefore, that it may be inferred that it was art that brought these two very gifted people together, and that it was his partnership with Fanny that helped develop MacIan's artistic genius. From the dates given in Mac-Donald's poems it is evident that these two were married before 1836.

Fanny continued to exhibit a diversity of subjects— 1838 *Miss Maria B. Hawes;* 1840 *Katty Macane's Darlint;* 1841 *The Little Sick*

---

*Published later as *MacIan's Costumes of the Clans*.

Scholar; 1842 *The Two Children;* 1843 *The Empty Cradle;* 1844 *The Lesson;* 1846 *But Father Anselmo will never again Penance Impose on Ladie or Swaine;* 1847 *The Slave's Dream.*

During these years MacIan, too, exhibited at the Academy as well as illustrating Logan's text of *The Clans of the Scottish Highlands.* Among his exhibits were (1839) *A Highland Cateran,* and (1840) *The Covenanter's Wedding,* in which year he retired from the stage and concentrated on art. Of special interest to Inverness is his picture of Gillies MacBean defending the breach in the stone dyke, made by the Campbells at Culloden, against a large force of horse and foot, of whom he is required to have slain single-handed thirteen men and a horse.

MacIan's *Highlanders at Home,* with an account by Logan (1848), is a delightful collection of paintings of the Highland way of life he had known so intimately in his youth. In all, MacIan exhibited thirty-nine paintings in London — the last in 1847. He died at Hampstead on December 13, 1856.

By the time I had collected all this information I was more interested than ever in both Fanny and MacIan. Examination of their various paintings made it clear that they had influenced each other strongly and often worked together. It was as if they had enjoyed some particularly close artistic relationship. There was such a mingling of ideas in both form and composition.

Out of the blue I got confirmation of this. I received a package with a note attached — "I picked this up in a saleroom. It's a MacDonald print. I thought you might like to have it."

Imagine my surprise when I unrolled the package and found myself looking at a print made from a picture which could have been painted by MacIan, but which had undoubtedly been painted by Fanny, for it bore her signature. It depicted Alaster MacDonald of Glencoe, sword in hand, with his wife, child and faithful hound beside him, fighting off several of Argyle's men on the night of the massacre of Glencoe in 1692. There was the stage-like elegance of the setting; the supple, well-proportioned figures, and the enthusiastic Highland appeal. But, whereas MacIan's paintings — whose subjects were almost invariably taken from Scottish history and treated with great vigour and earnestness — were always historically, meticulously correct, Fanny's in this case, at any rate, as I shall show, was woefully incorrect.

It is common knowledge that Alaster MacDonald and his

brother had been warned of the pre-arranged attack by a servant, and had successfully escaped into the hills before the actual massacre took place. Again, Alaster MacDonald in the picture, wears a Glengarry bonnet — a modern bonnet — which had come into fashion around 1800. The soldiers of Argyle's regiment look suspiciously like Cromwell's soldiers as depicted by MacIan himself in his MacMillan plate in *The Clans of the Scottish Highlands*.

The picture — undated — was dedicated by permission to the Chisholm of Chisholm — her esteemed patron. This was Duncan MacDonald Chisholm, who died in London on September 14, 1858 aged forty-seven — so this picture had been painted before that date. He had been a foremost member of the Highland Society of London.

The more I looked at the picture, though puzzled, the more I liked it. It was fired with such sincere enthusiasm for the Highlander — for her husband's ancestors who had suffered so terribly on that awful night. She had introduced her husband's dress, his bearing, his courage.

Little by little the conviction grew on me that this was her mind's eye picture of what MacIan would have done had he been confronted with that situation on that night. Suddenly I understood. At last I was face to face with MacIan! This was her memorial to him. He was no longer there to advise her historically when she painted it — but what did details matter? It was the man who had been taken from her she wanted to paint — MacIan, the man she had loved.

As I replaced *The Mountain Heath* on its shelf, I felt sure I now knew all I wished to know about R. R. MacIan.

Chapter 21

The Sobieski Riddle

THOUGH it was generally assumed that the direct Stuart line died out with Charles Edward and his brother, Cardinal York, there was a mystery about the matter which has only been solved within the last few years. The mystery centred round two handsome young men, John and Charles Allen. In 1816 they came to London from the Continent. They told how they had served with the French Army — fought at Dresden, Leipzig and Waterloo — the younger claiming to have received the Grand Cross of the Legion of Honour for gallantry from Napoleon himself.

What was more startling, however, was their statement that a secret — from what source they did not divulge — had been revealed to them about 1811, that they were directly descended from the exiled Stuarts, and therefore the heirs of the male Stuart line. To prove the authenticity of their claim they exhibited several Stuart relics — but what most impressed those who met them was the striking resemblance John bore to the Vandyke portrait of Charles I.

By 1820 their father, Thomas Allen, afterwards Thomas Hay Allan, and subsequently James Stuart, Count d'Albanie, paid the first of his frequent visits to Scotland, where rumour circulated freely, that he was a legitimate son of Prince Charles.

The parentage of this Thomas Allen was something of a mystery. He was reputed to be the son of Admiral Carter Allen, who in turn claimed descent from an early Earl Hay, of the Hays of Erroll. There were certain doubts, however, on this point — for though details of the birth of the Admiral's younger son John were easily procured, none could be found concerning Thomas. Furthermore, when Admiral Allen died in 1800, he bequeathed £2200 to John — but only £100 to Thomas. For these reasons it was thought that Thomas was an adopted son of the Admiral, who had been twice married.

Thomas and John Allen both entered the Navy. Third Lieutenant Thomas Allen was described as a tall, handsome, well-educated man, of quiet, rather studious demeanour. Although left only £100 by Admiral Allen, he was thought to have considerable independent means from some extraneous source. A somewhat elusive and restless individual, he resided sometimes in Britain, sometimes at Versailles and Boulogne-sur-mer, in France, and sometimes in Italy. In 1792 he married the very wealthy twenty-seven-year-old Miss Catherine Matilda Manning, and in 1798, leaving the Navy, settled in France, where it was believed one at least of his three children by this lady was born. These children were John, Charles Edward and Catherine Matilda. He died in London in 1852.

His sons, John and Charles Allen, showed their enthusiasm for things Scottish shortly after their arrival in London, by studying Gaelic there, under the tuition of Donald MacPherson. Apt pupils, they ultimately became so proficient that they could speak, read and write the language and even compose in it. A few years later they changed their names to what they considered was the more Scottish spelling, Allan, and having prefixed the name Hay, presented themselves as John Hay Allan and Charles Stuart Hay Allan. This was a strange mistake on their part, the original Allen being the correct spelling of the name, when used in connection with the Hay of Erroll family, and suggests their complete lack of documentary evidence when making the change.

In 1822 Charles married Mrs Anne Gardiner, a widow, youngest daughter of the Earl of Tyrone's second son. She was ten years his senior and had an income of £1000 per annum.

Although still residing in London, the brothers paid many visits to Scotland, living sometimes in Edinburgh, and sometimes, especially John, in the West Highlands. In Edinburgh they were commonly known as "The Princes," and occupied rooms in an upper flat at No. 1 Castle Street. They moved freely in the highest social circles, and regularly attended Mass in what is now St Mary's Cathedral.

In 1826 they moved to Morayshire. Here they dwelt for about three years at Windy Hills — latterly Milton Brodie, in the parish of Alves — and then moved to Logie, in the parish of Edinkillie, where they remained until 1838.

During this year they moved again, and settled eventually at Eilean Aigas, Beauly. Here, in the River Glass, near Kilmorack, is a small picturesque island on which Lord Lovat had erected a

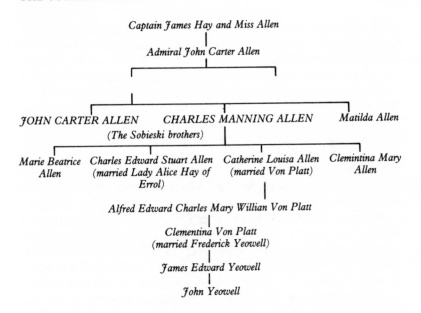

Captain James Hay and Miss Allen
|
Admiral John Carter Allen

JOHN CARTER ALLEN   CHARLES MANNING ALLEN   Matilda Allen
(The Sobieski brothers)

Marie Beatrice   Charles Edward Stuart Allen   Catherine Louisa Allen   Clemintina Mary
Allen   (married Lady Alice Hay of   (married Von Platt)   Allen
                  Errol)

Alfred Edward Charles Mary Willian Von Platt
|
Clementina Von Platt
(married Frederick Yeowell)
|
James Edward Yeowell
|
John Yeowell

handsome house, built to their own design, as their residence.

It had been suggested that Lord Lovat had done this out of loyalty for the house of Stuart. Lord Lovat may, however, have had quite a different reason for his generosity. Sir Simon Fraser, the Patriot — most renowned of all Fraser chiefs — had two daughters, the elder of whom married Sir Hugh Hay. Neidpath Castle, Peebleshire, was part of her dowry. On the keystone of the courtyard archway the strawberries (Fraser crest) appear in the crest of the Hays, symbolising the link between these two families. Family duty, as Lord Lovat considered it, towards the Hays, may have inspired the action.

At this date the name Hay Allan was relegated to obscurity, and the brothers blossomed out as John Sobieski Stolberg Stuart, Count d'Albanie, and Charles Edward Stuart, in spite of the fact that their father, also styled James Stuart, Count d'Albanie, was still alive. (Comte d'Albanie was the title used by Prince Charles after his father's death.)

At Eilean Aigaš they remained for about eight years, surrounded by their vast collection of Highland antiquities. Mrs Smith of Baltiboys gives an interesting picture of the brothers at that time.

"And we had those strange brothers, whose real name I can't remember, but they one day announced that they were Stuarts, lineally descended from Prince Charles, out of respect to whose wife, who never had a child, the elder brother assumed the name of John Sobieski . . . The mother was Scotch; her people had been in the service of the unfortunate Stuarts in Italy. Her sons were handsome men. They always wore the Highland dress, and looked melancholy, and spoke at times mysteriously. Half the clans in the Highlands believed in them."

In 1845 John Sobieski Stolberg Stuart, Count d'Albanie as "The Chevalier" John Sobieski Stuart, married Miss Georgina Kendall, daughter of Edward Kendall of Austrey, Warwickshire, of an old and somewhat moneyed family, and brought her to live at Eilean Aigas.

A year later, however, both brothers and their wives left this retreat, and ultimately settled in Austria-Hungary. The reason given for this exodus from Scotland was their desire to be near Charles's son, now an officer in the Austrian Army. The real reason, it was thought, was because of an anonymous attack attributed to Professor Skene and the Rev. Dr Mackay on John's lately published *Vestiarium Scoticum*. This these pundits denounced as a forgery, and at the same time published the details of the Allen lineage of its author.

To this attack John Sobieski Stuart wrote a lengthy reply, published by Blackwood, in which he ably defended his work. He made no effort, however, to substantiate any claim to Stuart ancestry.

In Austria-Hungary they remained, living at Prague and Presburg, where they were treated with great honour, and their claim to Royal descent fully acceded, until 1868, when they again returned to London, residing in the West End. By this time Charles was a widower, and the father of four children — one son and three daughters — one of whom, Marie, accompanied him. John and his wife lived near, and both brothers spent most of their time reading and writing in The British Museum.

John died, without issue, in 1872, and was buried at Eskadale, Beauly. His widow died at Bath in 1888.

Charles, now left alone, continued to make London his home, varied by visits to the North and the Continent. Much reduced in circumstances, he became a lay-worker in the Society of St Vincent de Paul, visiting the poor and sick, and giving of the little he had to those in need.

In 1880 he journeyed to Biarritz, and died on board ship, before returning to England. He, too, was eventually interred at Eska-dale. The tombstone over the grave of the brothers bears the following epitaph composed by Father Colin Grant, who was priest at Eskadale during the years the brothers lived there.

I.H.S. Hic requiescant in Domino Johannes Sobieski Stolberg Stuart, Comte D'Albanie, Natus XIV Junii MDCCXCVII., Mor-tuus XIII Feb. MDCCCLXXII et Carolus Eduardus Stuart, Comte D'Albanie, Natus IV Junii MDCCXCIX, Mortuus XXV Dec. MDCCCLXXX. R.I.P

Behind them the Sobieski Stuarts left several able literary works: *The Bridal of Caolchairn and other Poems*, by John Hay Allan, London 1822. *Vestiarium Scoticum with an Introduction & Notes*, by John Sobieski Stuart, Edinburgh 1842. *The Costume of the Clans*, by John Sobieski and Charles Edward Stuart, Edinburgh 1843. *Tales of the Century*, by John Sobieski and Charles Edward Stuart, Edinburgh 1847. *Lays of the Deer Forest*, by John Sobieski and Charles Edward Stuart, Edinburgh 1848. *Poems* by Charles Edward Stuart, London 1869.

In spite of much speculation and research, that is as much as was generally known until recently of the history and background of the two brothers. In 1952, however, a series of articles published by Mr C. L. Berry in *Notes and Queries*, made certain new assertions about the Allen family. These articles were compiled from a collection of Allen letters, which were lent by a descendant who had inherited them. They throw much light on the private history of Thomas Allen and his first family, and assert the following facts.

John Carter Allen (alias John Hay Allan; alias John Sobieski Stolberg Stuart, Count d'Albanie) was born at Newton, Oyster-mouth, Glamorgan, Wales, on 4th August 1795.

Charles Manning Allen (alias Charles Edward Stuart, Count d'Albanie) was born sometime in April 1797.

Matilda Allen, their sister, was born at Oystermouth, South Wales, on 18th October 1799.

If we accept this information then the Christian names, sur-names, and dates of birth on the tombstone at Eskadale Chur-chyard are incorrect.

References to ages in their own poems prove Mr Berry's dates correct, and we realise the brothers were named after their grandfather, Admiral John Carter Allen and their uncle, The Rev. Charles Manning.

They were the children, by his first wife, of Thomas Allen — who, the writer insists, never styled himself James Stuart, Count d'Albanie. This name and title were used only by his sons when referring to their father, who was born on 7th May, 1767, almost five years before Prince Charles first met his bride. No further evidence is needed to disprove the claim that Thomas Allen was the legitimate son of Prince Charles.

Thomas Allen is also stated to have been indeed the elder son of Admiral Carter Allen. Why the Admiral should have left him only £100 in his will, drawn up about six months before his death in 1800, is not disclosed. It may have been because he considered this son's circumstances sufficiently affluent after his marriage in 1792 to the very wealthy Catherine Matilda Manning.

Mr and Mrs Thomas Allen spent the early years of their married life in Glamorgan, where their three children were born. In 1812 he was living in Bagshot, and from this date moved around frequently. After the death of his first wife (about 1810) he speculated disastrously with both his own and his children's money. In 1816 he was involved in a law suit in Chancery. About this date he and his family moved to Boulogne — perhaps because of his debts — and remained there, on and off, until 1829. During the last thirteen years of his life he hid his identity by adopting his second wife's maiden name of Salmon. He died, intestate, leaving only debts behind him, and was buried at Old St Pancras Churchyard as Captain Thomas Hay Allen, R.N.

From this it is apparent that the Sobieski brothers' claims to battle honours from Napoleon were sheer "moonshine".

Mr C. L. Berry is of opinion that the Allens were English — but Mr A. G. Williamson — author of "The Ninth James Stuart" — prefers to think of them as Scottish. From what he writes it is possible to deduce that Thomas Allen, father of the two brothers was actually a Hay, his grandfather having been a Captain James Hay, who fought with the rebel brother of James, Earl of Erroll, in the Forty-Five. This Captain Hay is said to have married an Irish lady, a Miss Allen, who inherited both property and money, in consequence of which he dropped his own name, and assumed that of his wife.

This latter information is interesting in view of the fact that in 1874 Charles Sobieski Stuart's son, Charles Edward, married

Lady Alice Hay, daughter of the Earl of Erroll — an alliance which showed that the Hays of Erroll, far from being averse to the Allen claim of Hay descent, approved it. Lord Lovat's friendship with the Sobieski Stuarts also assumes its true significance. The Hays of Erroll had been members of the Court of the Stuarts from the time of James II — and who knows, over the generations, but that Hays and Stuarts may have had clandestine alliances and offspring of which the general public knew little or nothing? In fact this very possibility may have inspired the Sobieski bogus claim to definite Stuart ancestry, and would allow that they may have had a trickle of Stuart blood in their veins.

Lady Alice Hay's mother — a Fitzclarence — was a natural daughter of William IV by Mrs Jordan. If perchance, Lady Alice Hay's husband, Charles Edward Stuart, was indeed descended from a Stuart, an amazing union took place in which the two great opposing houses of Guelph and Stuart were united by natural descendants.

There was no issue of this marriage, but the Allen line was continued by Catherine Louisa Allen, one of the three daughters of Charles Manning Allen. Born in 1827, she married Edle Eduard Von Platt, Colonel Austrian Imperial Life Guards, who died in 1897. After the death of her brother and her two sisters, she became the sole representative of her father, Charles Manning Allen. She died in Vienna in 1900, having issue of one son, Alfred Edward Charles Mary William Von Platt, who was born on the 15th December 1861. This gentleman was twice married, and had one daughter by each wife. These were Clementina Von Platt, and Maria Stuart Von Platt. The latter married Dr Henry Thon on 5th November, 1940.

Clementina Von Platt, who was born in 1882, married Frederick Yeowell in 1898. She died in 1913, and her husband in 1918. There was issue of the marriage from which her grandson, John Yeowell, is descended and, according to an article in *The British American Chronicle*, "is the first to pour scorn on a long demolished claim."

Chapter 22

The Highland Railway

IN a comparatively small country like Britain a unified system of control of the railways is probably inevitable, and in many ways desirable. Yet the loss of a separate identity and of local control cannot but leave certain regrets. The host of little railways, so much the planners' nightmare, was each one a symbol of local pride and enterprise. Each of them was "our railway," and of none was this more true than of the small companies who came to form the Highland Railway, in its time to become the L.M.S., and at last to be swallowed up by British Railways. Family associations extending over many years have invested the "Highland" with special claims on my regard, but my reasons for writing about it are not entirely personal. Even today, in a much reduced state, it is considered by many, chiefly on account of the mountainous terrain it traverses, to be the most interesting component of British Railways.

It was in the early forties of last century that the people of Inverness became affected with "Railway Fever". Great things had been done in England during the previous thirty years in the way of making railways, and the resulting expansion of trade was astonishing. Leading Inverness citizens felt that they could no longer be content with the hardships of travelling over hundreds of miles of mountainous country by stage-coach, or the slow, monotonous voyage of the coasting steamer.

There was a widespread desire for something more modern than "The Caledonian" — a stage-coach which needed considerably over two days for the journey between Inverness and Perth, or a similar vehicle requiring a whole week for the journey from Inverness to Edinburgh.

These journeyings, as well as being very tedious, were also quite expensive, as a study of a few of their fares illustrates: Inverness to Aberdeen — inside the coach, £2, outside, £1 2s; Inverness to Edinburgh — inside the coach £2 5s, outside, £1 12s; Inverness to

Thurso — inside the coach £2 11s 6d, outside, £1 17s 6d; Inverness to Tain — inside the coach £1, outside, 14s. Trains were running in England — covering long distances at great speed — and much more cheaply. Trains must run in the Highlands, too!

Accordingly, in 1845 a proposal was submitted to a Parliamentary Committee for a railway from Inverness to Perth. The route selected was identical with that used by the stage-coaches — across the Monadhliadh and Grampian ranges, through passes 1323 feet and 1484 feet respectively above sea-level. The engineer who was the moving spirit of the projected railway, and put forward the plans for crossing the Grampians, was an Invernessian — Joseph Mitchell — and so ridiculous was the scheme thought, that not only was the Bill thrown out, but Mr Mitchell was held to ridicule for proposing it. In the light of what followed, it is interesting to quote part of the speech of the opposing counsel in the debate:

"Ascending such a summit as 1450 feet was very unprecedented, and Mr Mitchell, the engineer, was the greatest mountain climber he had heard of. He beat Napoleon outright, and quite eclipsed Hannibal. He read a book the other day, of several hundred pages, describing how Hannibal crossed the Alps, but after this line will have passed, he had no doubt quartos would be written about Mr Mitchell!"

Nothing daunted, the Highland people determined to tackle their project in their own way, and on the 21st September 1854, the first sod of what was to become The Highland Railway was cut in Inverness. This had been made possible by the whole-hearted loyalty and magnanimity of the people of Inverness and district, who had raised the magnificent sum of £80,000, the capital required for the construction of the first part of the railway, the section, fifteen and a half miles long, from Inverness to Nairn.

The scheme was inaugurated with true Highland spirit. The day was observed as a holiday in the town, and a crowd of over 8000 people turned out to see the procession which did honour to the occasion and the ceremony of cutting the first sod.

On Monday, 5th November 1855 — a little more than a year later — the line between Inverness and Nairn was ready for traffic, and the occasion was signalised by the running of an excursion train from Inverness to Nairn and back.

This was another great day in the history of Inverness, and more than half the population gathered in the railway station, which was resplendent with waving flags and bunting.

From then onwards small companies of enterprising citizens formed themselves into groups, each group making itself responsible for the laying of a certain mileage of railway line which passed through the county in which the group had its headquarters.

In 1857 a new length of line was acquired by the process of amalgamation. By this time the Inverness and Aberdeen Railway — a separate company from the Inverness and Nairn — were nearing completion of their line, and it was decided that these companies be amalgamated. Thus the Inverness and Nairn Company now ran between Inverness and Aberdeen.

By 1861 the dream of Mr Joseph Mitchell, which had been so openly scorned, came into being. A company was formed under the title of the Inverness and Perth Junction to construct a line from Forres up through Strathspey, and over the Grampians into the valley of the Tay, where it joined and took over a railway which had been formed to Dunkeld, with a branch from Ballinluig to Aberfeldy. Mr Mitchell had the satisfaction of being the engineer of this line which was constructed more rapidly than any other railway in the kingdom, while it reached the highest altitude yet attained in Britain — 1484 feet.

The Inverness and Aberdeen Junction Company extended their line from Invergordon to Bonar Bridge in 1864; the Skye line from Dingwall to Stromeferry was opened in 1870; the Sutherland Railway from Bonar Bridge to Golspie in 1868; the Duke of Sutherland's Railway from Golspie to Helmsdale in 1871; and the Sutherland and Caithness Railway from Helmsdale to Wick and Thurso in 1874.

By 1884, a mere thirty years after the cutting of the first turf in Inverness, the several small railway companies had been amalgamated under the euphonious and comprehensive title of the Highland Railway — a railway which ran to Aberdeen in the east, to Wick and Thurso in the north, to Kyle of Lochalsh in the west, and to Perth in the south. It is more than interesting in view of the different ideas held today on the subject of private enterprise to examine how this was made possible. The capital expenditure on the Dingwall and Skye Railway at the date of amalgamation in 1880 amounted to £311,957. The ordinary shareholders agreed to sacrifice one half of their holdings, and to ask for no dividend prior to that date.

No dividend was paid during the first seven years of the

Sutherland Railway Company, whose capital amounted to £211,852, and an exchange was affected at the rate of 60 per cent of Highland Railway Stock when the amalgamation took place.

The Duke of Sutherland parted with his railway, which cost him £72,182, at a discount of 13 per cent.

The Sutherland and Caithness Railway, costing £433,266, was taken over by the Highland Railway at a discount of 50 per cent, and the shareholders received no dividend.

So eager were all shareholders to have the different amalgamations carried through, and the railway run as a complete entity in order that it might serve their country in the very highest degree, that on learning after amalgamation that £1,200,000 was still required to open and equip the new Highland Railway for traffic, they did not hesitate to set about raising this further amount. Thirty-two of the shareholders paid in full the sum of £872,773, in gifts ranging from £355,545 to £2000. To realise the balance required the directors gave their own personal security to the banks and insurance offices the whole of them becoming, thus, jointly and severally, responsible for the amount. The obligation continued for ten years, but in consequence of the steady development of the traffic, it was ultimately discharged without the directors losing a single sixpence. Thus native courage and determination won the day in the greatest industrial event which ever took place in Highland history.

Even after all financial difficulties had been overcome the running of the Highland Railway, mainly owing to the difficult country it traversed, proved no sinecure. Many were the problems that the Highlanders had to grapple with, including rivers swollen by fierce mountain torrents and subsequent landslides, but the arch-enemy was snow.

Severe storms of this sort occurred frequently in the early days of the railway, especially it seemed during the Christmas holiday season. In 1881 the "snow fiend" excelled himself. A snowblock at Dava lasted for five consecutive days. One train was entombed on the north side of the station, and another met a similar fate at Huntly's Cave on the other side. The staff crawled in and out of the office by means of an improvised tunnel through the snow. The snow wreaths were over twenty feet high, and with the wind roaring round the Knock the drift was simply blinding.

Pilot engines with heavy snowploughs were despatched to try to force a passage to the snowed-up trains, but all attempts were

fruitless. To witness a snowplough engine at full speed charging a
drift is something not soon to be forgotten. Huge blocks of snow
shoot about 50 feet into the air, and as they fall with a dull crash the
sound resembles distant thunder.

While some parts of the line were blocked for miles, other parts
had only a covering of about an inch of snow. As soon as the
drifting had ceased, the engineer and a squad of men approached
the snowblock on the north side, and an attempt was made to cut
out the entombed train. It was a weary struggle, and the engineer
had frequently to call a halt for refreshments to keep up the hearts
of the men. To add to the difficulties, telegraph communication
was interrupted, and for a time trains were leaving Perth on
schedule, with the result that passengers were subsequently held
up in waiting rooms, station houses, or anywhere they could find
accommodation.

The Superintendent of Line, accompanied by a telegraph oper-
ator, managed to transfer the headquarters of the Highland
Railway from Inverness to one of the snowed-up railway carriages.
Proceeding on horseback, having previously travelled from Inverness via Elgin and Speyside, they rode along the line until they
came to the rear of the buried train at "Huntly's Cave". A passage
was cut through the snow to enable them to enter a first-class
carriage. A telegraph wire was then "tapped", and a connection
led through the roof-light aperture. They were thus able to get in
touch with the south line.

Paradoxical as it may appear, however, even this worst of all
snowblocks had its lighter side, and a certain well-to-do Manches-
ter merchant swore it was much the happiest experience he had
ever had. The reason was, of course, a lady, in the person of a
bonnie Caithness lassie. They met in a snowed-up carriage, and on
a journey that lasted quite a week, found each other's company so
pleasing that the merchant "popped the question", and both lived
to bless the "snow fiend" as their best friend!

In spite of all difficulties, the Highland Railway continued to
flourish, for it was manned by a body of workers whose record of
unselfish service will never be beaten. Let us remember a few.

There was K, the ticket collector. Even when well up in years,
he was one of the most alert and active of men. It was no unusual
thing for him to check trains while in motion, in order to save time.
To understand the full import of this, one must realise that
corridor carriages were unknown in the early days. Daily he could

be seen passing along the footboards from one end of the train to the other while trains were crossing the Ness Viaduct. In his early days he had been an accomplished acrobat and gymnast.

Next to the stationmaster, perhaps the most worried and harassed official on Inverness platform was the station policeman. His duties, when considered, amounted to one eternal round of drudgery from early morning till late at night, and yet he performed them all with light-hearted cheerfulness. To enumerate his many tasks would be well-nigh impossible, but the following were a few of them. In addition to ordinary police supervision of the platform, the sidings, the goods shed, etc, he attended at the post office in the High Street every mail, brought down all head office and other letters, sorted and delivered them. Not only so, but he made two or three calls at these offices every day in order to collect all letters for the outgoing mails. He had to ring a bell five minutes before the departure of each train, north and south, and close the two front doors of the station just as the starting whistle was blown. Furthermore, he was responsible for the posting up of the company's advertising bills, including holiday bills, at the station, and had to prove himself more or less a walking encyclopaedia of ready information to satisfy the questioning strangers and local people whose interest in the railway helped to make it such a success.

The locomotive superintendent, Mr Stroudley, was a man of rare genius. All his leisure he devoted to inventing, and quite a number of inventions bear his name. The most important of these is "Stroudley's Ramps", a pair of which may still be found at every station along the line, and in every guard's van, and have proved invaluable in cases of derailed vehicles.

If the Highland Railway was unique in Britain because of the country it traversed, it was unique, too, for the speed attained over this type of country. Much of the railroad was only single track, and although the locomotives had begun modestly with a speed of about twenty miles an hour, they became so immensely improved that within fifty years there operated a real express service carrying unusually heavy loads, often quoted as reaching 375 tons.

It is true that speeds did not average fifty or sixty miles per hour — the express speeds of that day — but with frequent grades of 1 in 70 or 80, and branch sections of 1 in 60 or 1 in 50, this could hardly be expected. Yet its schedule reveals long, non-stop runs of 35¼ miles between Perth and Blair Atholl — all single track, except the 7¼ miles over Caledonian metals — booked in 52 and 55 minutes in the harder direction, and in 51 minutes — this including a stop at Perth ticket platform — in the easier direction.

For the mountain section of 36¼ miles from Blair Atholl to Kingussie in the harder direction we find 61 minutes allowed, and in the south or easier direction 54 minutes. The 68¼-mile run from Perth to Newtonmore, including a stop at Blair Atholl for water, took 114 minutes, while the "winter season" express from Perth to Kingussie completed its journey in 111 minutes. Aviemore to Inverness, 34¾ miles, required 54 minutes; Inverness to Tain, a distance of 44 miles, 64 minutes, and Helmsdale to Georgemas, 45¾ miles, 73 minutes.

Because of the heavy loads and exceptional grades, considerable use of "assisting" engines had to be made. For this purpose "tank" engines were introduced, and used in the working of the lines from Blair Atholl to Dalnaspidal (1422 feet above sea level), from Inverness to Slochd Crossing, from Kingussie to Dalnaspidal, from Aviemore to Slochd Crossing, from Forres to Dava or to Alves, and from Helmsdale to Altnabreac.

The secret of the maintenance of relatively high average speeds lay in the provision of apparatus for exchanging "tablets" on single line sections without slackening, often at a speed of 60 miles per hour; of the alignment of passing loops so that wherever possible the high-speed direction had a straight run through, and of good unaided engine work on the moderately hard sections — and with medium loads, even on the very difficult ones.

It was this "express" nature of the Highland Line, and the willing co-operation of all workers, that made it possible in two world wars for a huge and unprecedented military, naval and general traffic to be carried, often over a single line, without loss or mishap. Thus were the Highlands enabled to play their part to the full in these great struggles for freedom — a part made possible by the enterprise, energy and magnanimity of a former patriotic and public-spirited generation.

Chapter 23

The Highland Capital

INVERNESS — the mouth of the Ness. It is a simple, pictures-que name, derived as far as can be ascertained from an old Gaelic term "INBHIR" meaning the mouth. Yet, in its natural simplic-ity, a name which conjures up visions of a place which enjoyed trade, strategic importance and, perchance, great antiquity.

Situated at the junction of the old trade routes from north to south, and east to west, Inverness has, from its earliest days, known outstanding strength and importance. Boethius and Buchanan concur in affirming that Inverness was founded by Evenus II, the fourteenth King of Scotland, who is thought to have died about 60 B.C. These two historians further aver that the site of the town was chosen on account of its advantageous position for commerce — and, at a later date this statement is repeated by another historian named Guthrie. By sea and land Inverness occupied a commanding position, being the gateway to the High-lands from the eastern sea, and guardian of land communications to the west and north. It is therefore, obvious, that on account of situation alone this town was bound to play a very important part in the life and history of the Highlands.

The numerous relics of very great antiquity existing around the town, however, point to its having been a populated stronghold at a much earlier age. Within the environs are the remains of a British hill fort at Craig Phadric, a Roman fort at Bona, and several sepulchral Cairns and Druidical circles — one, an almost perfect specimen on the estate of Leys. The early history of the town is more or less clouded in heavy mist — but from this almost crepuscular mirage one date emerges, authoritatively blazoning a real historical fact. In 565 A.D. St. Columba came from Ireland to Inverness — "ad ostiam Nessai", which, because of its outstand-ing situation was then the Capital of the Northern Pictish King-dom — and which has remained the Capital of the North of Scotland during all the fourteen successive centuries.

For several centuries after this visit of St. Columba to King Brude the Highlands were ruled from Inverness by Kings, and from this town, too, Macbeth and his predecessors later ruled the great semi-independent Province of Moray, which extended from the Dornoch Firth to the Spey, and westwards almost to the sea. In the twelfth century Inverness was firmly established as the seat of the Royal Government for the whole Highlands. A new Castle was erected on the present Castle Hill, to serve as the symbol and seat of power of the King of Scotland in the Highlands, and the town itself was created a Royal Burgh. The privilege of foreign trade was conferred on its burgesses alone, and thereafter the whole export trade of the North passed through its hands.

Thus from the mid-early days of the reign of King David I, after the defeat of the men of Moray, and the annexation of this province to the Crown, Inverness was, in a very real sense, the capital of the Highlands, and provided a substantial element in Scotland's stormy history during the following centuries. As a natural headquarters for the North of Scotland it enjoyed royal visits. Parliaments met there and armies, both Royal and Highland rallied their forces within its confines. All this made it the veritable heart of the Highlands — a heart whose animating and stimulating blood flowed freely into the surrounding country. Crofters from the near-by countryside responded to this fosterage by bringing their surplus produce to the ready market of the town, and here wool and skins changed hands for such luxuries as the town could offer.

This small, busy town, snuggling comfortably as it did almost around the base of its strong castle, enjoyed such peace and prosperity that it attracted those excellent Continental traders, the Flemings, to its gates, and by their help, a foreign trade was developed which proved not only an asset, but a credit, to the town. Disapproval of these foreigners and their trading practices, however, soon began to manifest itself all over Scotland, and the men of Moray were not slow to register their resentment. In 1160, the unsuccessful siege of Malcolm IV by Celtic Earls, in Perth, forced him to take drastic action in the matter, and, as Fordun, the historian, narrates, the result was that all the natives were scattered over Scotland, far from the locus of their birth, and the law-abiding strangers installed in their places.

Inverness must have augmented its population considerably on account of this influx of foreigners, for, at this date, the small township found it necessary to spread itself out. The first extension lay in the direction of Church Street, and the quay, which was situated just below the Maggot. The next was along where High Street now stands, towards the rough track which ran from the south to the north of Scotland, approaching Inverness by way of Kingsmills, and descending into the town near the Post Office steps, whence it wended its way by Hamilton Street and Academy Street to the ford at the Friars' Shott.

The native Scots, naturally, determined to oust the hated foreigners from their homes, and the capture of William the Lion at Alnwick, in July, 1174, and the consequent anarchy, provided them with the chance of revolt. In 1179, William the Lion — having regained his liberty, in December 1174, by agreeing to become Henry's vassal for Scotland — made his headquarters in Inverness, when, penetrating into Ross, he subdued that county and built the castles of Redcastle and Dunscaith.

In 1181, Donald Ban MacWilliam, a chief related to the King, aspiring to the Crown, invaded Moray. He held the Highlands for six years, but in 1187, William the Lion, attacked, defeated, and killed him in Badenoch, near Inverness, bringing his head in triumph into the town of Inverness, where it was fixed on the Castle "as a gazing stock to the whole army".

Nine years later William returned to Inverness in order to impose his sovereignty on the Norse Earl of Orkney, who held Caithness, and aimed at making it independent of Scotland. A year later this Earl advanced against Inverness in an effort to regain his power, but was totally defeated near the Castle. On hearing this news William hurriedly returned to Inverness, in order to "scour all these Highland districts", captured the Earl, and destroyed Thurso Castle. On three other occasions, William was forced to visit the Highland capital in order to deal with troubles in the North. To Inverness itself he gave at least three charters confirming the ancient privileges of the burgesses, and conferring on them several new ones.

Alexander II was crowned in 1214, and about a year later Ross rose in support of Donald MacWilliam — a son of Donald Ban MacWilliam — and Kenneth MacHeth. Ferchard Macintagart, Earl of Ross, quelled the rising, and presented the heads of these two insurgents to the King. In 1220, there was a great "hosting" at Inverness because of a rising led by one, Donald MacNeil.

In 1228, Inverness was destroyed for the first time in its history.

Gillescop Mahohegan, an extensive Badenoch landowner, was the instigator of this revolt. Some time previously, at Edinburgh, he had been admonished for failing to bring his hostages on an appointed day. His reaction to this indignity was rebellion — attacking and burning near-by forts, and setting fire to the greater part of the town of Inverness. He succeeded in holding out against a strong force for a few months, but was eventually captured and put to death.

It did not take long for the citizens of Inverness to rebuild their town, the houses being, at the time, built of wood. Thereafter followed a period of unbroken peace during which a rare culture influenced the life of the town. In 1233, the Dominican Friars received a grant of part of the land belonging to the Parish Church, from the Abbey of Arbroath, and in 1240, Alexander gifted them the Maggot — then an island — and other ground lying between the burial ground of the Parish Church and the wall of the Priory. The Dominicans' land, in all, extended to about six acres, and they also owned the fishing ground still known as the Friars' Shott.

The Priory — a handsome erection built between 1233 and 1240 — dominated the social life of the town and there, on occasion, even the King was entertained. The brethern, Mendicant Friars, wearing the white gown and scapular of their order, over which sometimes a black cloak with hood was thrown, were highly respected members of the community, spreading as they did their refinement and learning amongst the youth of the town.

Adhering to the policy of William the Lion, Alexander was wont, at this time, to make an annual circuit throughout the Sheriffdoms of Scotland. Most of these visits terminated at Inverness. To pay honour to the King and his nobles on these occasions, banquets, carousals and amusements were provided and enjoyed by all classes, and this gave a very special atmosphere and life to the town. During these inspections, the streets, gay with the panoply of knights, noblemen, their ladies and retainers, hummed with a flushed excitement. Hunting and hawking parties rode abroad to enjoy the sport of the near-by countryside, and castle, tavern, and the more opulent homes diffused the tempting waft of feast and wine, whilst the merry music of the carefree visitors and their hosts filled the air.

This pleasant state of affairs obtained in the town — which by 1240 had assumed the form which its principal streets present today — until 1262, when the rumble of war again disturbed the community.

After the Maid of Norway died, in September 1290, there were two claimants for the throne of Scotland — Bruce and Baliol. Each claimant had his own supporters, and these frequently engaged in conflict. When Baliol's supporters had laid waste the Crown lands in Moray, an appeal — long and anxiously awaited — was made to Edward I to intervene. Seizing his chance to interfere in the succession, Edward astutely directed that both claimants acknowledge his overlordship, submit their claims to his decision, and surrender all Royal Castles into his hands.

Among these was the Castle at Inverness. Sir William de Braytoft was appointed its governor. His salary of one mark per day — twice the amount paid to governors of other Northern Castles — emphasises the importance of Inverness Castle at this period. The castles in his power, Edward next insisted that all Church dignitaries, nobility, land-holders and burgesses should take an oath of allegiance to him, and for this purpose appointed Commissioners throughout Scotland. Inverness was the place chosen for the administration of his oath for all people of importance dwelling north of the Spey.

On 17th November, 1292, Edward awarded the Crown of Scotland to Baliol, and shortly afterwards all English garrisons were withdrawn from the Castles. For some time Baliol ruled in accordance with Edward's wishes, but finding this rein irksome, eventually defied him, in 1295. The result was war — a war in which Edward conquered all Scotland, and retired to the South in 1296, carrying with him the Coronation stone from Scone.

It was with the aid of the burgesses of Inverness that the first successful blow in the War of Independence was struck in 1297, when Andrew de Moray of Petty and Avoch, a near neighbour of the town, with Alexander Pilche, burgess of Inverness, as his chief lieutenant, led a revolt which liberated the north, and resulted in the Battle of Stirling Bridge, where Wallace and his army proved victors. Though Edward won the Battle of Falkirk a year later, this did not give him Scotland, as the Scottish barons set up a government of their own. In 1303, therefore, Edward determined on a final and complete conquest of Scotland. In a victorious march Northward he again captured Inverness Castle. Alexander Pilche, loyal citizen of Inverness and staunch supporter of Wallace, refused to swear fealty to him, and for this defiance lost his lands. In 1304, Stirling Castle fell, and in 1305, Wallace was betrayed and executed. Scotland seemed to lie completely conquered — but a few months later the torch of freedom began to flicker anew.

Bruce, crowned at Scone in 1306, gained some of his earliest and staunchest adherents from Inverness and its neighbourhood, and it was to this town he came in the crisis of his fate in the autumn of 1307, when the Independence of Scotland was secured on account of the immense strength he gathered together in and around the town. It was with Inverness as his base, and with an army drawn from the town and neighbourhood that he rallied the Highlands to his side, humbled the Earl of Ross, and in a succession of brilliant campaigns regained all Scotland north of the Forth and Clyde. It was this same army which took Edinburgh Castle, and later formed the van which routed the English cavalry attempting to relieve Stirling Castle on the eve of the Battle of Bannockburn, in 1314. In 1312, Bruce had come to Inverness to meet the ambassadors of the King of Norway in order to ratify "The Annual of Norway", the treaty entered into between the Kings of Scotland and Norway in 1266, and to settle various other matters outstanding between the two nations. Alexander Pilche, as might be expected, was one of Bruce's followers, and was rewarded for his devotion by being made Sheriff of Inverness.

In 1369, Bruce's son, David II, journeyed to Inverness to receive the submission of John, Lord of the Isles. Forty-two years later John's son, Donald, came to Inverness, where, having collected an army of islanders en route, he was joined by many Highland chiefs and their clans, on his way to "the Red Harlaw", fought near Aberdeen. Here he was defeated by the Earl of Mar, who afterwards travelled north to Inverness to rebuild the Castle, and thence rule the Highlands.

In 1427, James I visited Inverness to hold Parliament and restore law and order in the Highlands. On this occasion the Lord of the Isles and several other Highland chiefs were imprisoned in the town. During the remainder of the fifteenth century, in the wars between the Crown and the Lords of the Isles, Inverness was burned and sacked four times. Eventually, in 1509, the Earl of Huntly was appointed as Hereditary Sheriff and Keeper of the Castle, with orders for its extension and strengthening. From here the Highlands and Islands were ruled in the King's name.

In 1562, Queen Mary came to Inverness on that famous visit which brought to a head the differences between her and the Earl of Huntly, and resulted in the defeat and death of Huntly at the

Battle of Corrichie some weeks after her arrival. It was during this period that she resided in a house in Bridge Street until the Governor of the Castle, who insisted on holding it for Lord Gordon, son of the Earl of Huntly, was forced to capitulate. For his disobedience the governor was hung over his own battlements. In 1591, James VI, Queen Mary's son, granted "the Golden Charter" to the town — a charter which confirmed all the old rights and liberties to the Burgh.

Once again, in the Civil Wars of the seventeenth century, Inverness, as the rallying place of the armies of the Covenant in the Highlands, became a centre of turbulence, when it resisted the siege of Montrose. It was the chief sufferer in the two short risings of February and April, 1649, the first of which resulted in the execution of the Marquis of Huntly, and the second in the defeat of the rebels at the Battle of Balveny. It was through Inverness that Montrose was led southwards after his defeat at Carbisdale, and his capture a few days later in August.

A regiment of Cromwell's army arrived at Inverness in November, 1651, and from then until the Restoration, it formed the headquarters of his government in the Highlands. So important did Cromwell consider the town that he built a fortress at the mouth of the river to check attacks from the north. This fortress, said to have cost £80,000 and taken five years to build, had accommodation for a thousand men. At the request of the Highland chiefs it was demolished after the Restoration. The clock tower, however, is still to be seen today.

The Revolution brought further trouble to Inverness. Macdonald of Keppoch, taking advantage of the general unrest, raided the MacKintosh country, and attempted to sack Inverness. Dundee, on his way north to raise the Highlands for James, found the MacDonalds furiously attacking the town. He cleverly persuaded the townspeople to buy Keppoch off, and led the Macdonalds away to serve in his campaign, which ended at Killiecrankie.

After the Act of Union of 1707 Inverness chose to support the Jacobites. When the Earl of Mar raised the standard in 1715, King James was proclaimed at the Market Cross, and the Castle seized and garrisoned by his supporters. Two months later, however, the exiled Lord Lovat, returned, raised his clan in support of the Hanoverian house, and, joining the Grants, forced the garrison to abandon the Castle.

The Forty-Five found Inverness stoutly Jacobite, and when

Prince Charles took up residence in the town, two months before
Culloden, he was accorded a royal welcome. During the previous
six months, when the Prince was advancing on England, Inverness had been held by the Hanoverians, who, on attempting a
surprise attack on the Prince at Moy, on 16th February, 1746,
were routed by a gallant blacksmith and his six companions —
though two thousand strong. Two days later the Prince advanced
on the town which had been hastily evacuated by the Hanoverians,
who had left only a small force to garrison the Castle. A few days
later the town fell to the Prince, who ordered the Castle to be
blown up. By 1820, all signs of its ruins even had disappeared. The
Battle of Culloden sealed the doom of the Jacobites — and thus,
for the second time in Scottish history, the fate of Scotland was
decided in the vicinity of Inverness.

On that memorable day, the 16th of April, 1746, a party of
Argyleshire Militia, disguised as followers of the Prince, anticipat-
ing the defeat of the Highlanders, marched into the town, and
taking possession of the eastern approach to the bridge, locked the
gates, and ranged themselves round them with drawn claymores.

The Battle lost, the Highlanders rushed into the town in an
effort to escape to the hills of Stratherrick and Loch Ness by way of
Bridge Street and the Bridge. The militia immediately obstructed
their escape, and, owing to the narrowness of Bridge Street — a
mere alleyway running between houses all approached by projecting turn-pike stairs — the state of affairs became chaotic, and it
seemed as though all the Highlanders must be trapped. It was then
that Dr Fraser, of the family of Reelig, who had been fighting with
the Prince, shouted, "My God, men, will you stand here and be
butchered? Do you not hear the bugles of the King's troopers at
the other end of the town?" Claymore in hand, and followed by the
Highlanders, he rushed against the Argyleshire Militia, cut them
down, and forcing the locked gates, gained for the Highlanders
the route of retreat.

During the years which followed the Forty-Five, Inverness
completely changed its character. Trade supplanted war, and the
town began to acquire its modern aspect. The stormy incidents of
the past had left scarce a vestige of its ancient buildings — but new
edifices were taking their places. The Castle was once again rebuilt
in 1834. To facilitate trade, the Caledonian Canal, forming an
unbroken waterway from Inverness to Fort William, was opened
in 1822.

The most disastrous floods ever witnessed in the north were experienced in January, 1849, when the seven-arched stone bridge over the River Ness, built in 1684, was swept away, and the waters of the river rushed out and completely submerged the near-by low-lying areas for fully three days.

Exactly one hundred years after the Forty-Five a proposal was submitted to a Parliamentary Committee for a railway, to run from Inverness to Perth. The route selected was identical with that used by the stage-coaches, across the Monadhliadh and Grampian ranges. The engineer who put forward plans for this enterprise was an Invernessian — Joseph Mitchell. So impossible was the scheme considered, that not only was the Bill thrown out, but Mr Mitchell held to ridicule for proposing it — the opposing counsel scornfully comparing him with Hannibal crossing the Alps!

In spite of this derision Inverness was "en fete" on the 21st September, 1854, when the first sod of what eventually became the Highland Railway was cut by the Countess of Seafield. Thirty years later Inverness was the headquarters of a railway which ran to Keith in the east, to Wick and Thurso in the north, to Kyle of Lochalsh in the west, and to Perth in the south.

The building of the Cameron Barracks at Millburn was commenced in 1883, and this was followed by the erection of a Drill Hall in Rose Street, in 1885. On July 24th, 1889, the Cameron Highlanders' monument — a handsome statue of a Cameron Highlander in review order — was unveiled by Cameron of Lochiel. The site for this memorial had occasioned some controversy amongst the townspeople, some favouring the Castle Hill, for from here the soldier would have looked towards Lochaber, the cradle of the regiment. The weight of opinion, however, declared for the Station Square, where, standing in the very thick of the town's activity, the monument would be a constant memorial not only of the gallant dead of this great regiment who fell in Egypt and the Sudan, but of the military associations of the town.

Today, midst all the bustle of its modern, busy streets, Inverness may be said to have faithfully retained that same character which its simple name suggested. It is still Capital of the Highlands.